WALKING THROUGH THE WRECKAGE

OBSERVATIONS ON LIFE
AND OTHER ABOMINATIONS

Printed in the United States of America

First Printing, 2015

ISBN 978-0-9962632-0-7

Cover illustration by Marcello Vargas Machuca

For all the disappointed, demoralized, and weary;
to all of life's failures and flops...
you know who you are.

TABLE OF CONTENTS

WALKING THROUGH THE WRECKAGE

OBSERVATIONS ON LIFE
AND OTHER ABOMINATIONS

ALEXIOS

INTRODUCTION

I, ALEXIOS

I pushed Caesar across the Rubicon and spoon-fed Moses the story of the burning bush. With simply a well-placed whisper or a perfectly-timed suggestion, I sent Hannibal and his elephants up and over the Alps, I toppled the mighty city of Constantinople as the cathedral bells rang out one final time, and I rained revolution down on France. After inciting World War I, I didn't pause for a moment's rest before instigating its sequel, and I schooled both Goebbels and Churchill on the art of the Big Lie. History's greatest calamities and deceptions bear my cold, dead fingerprint. Call me what you wish – scourge of civilization, bane of humanity, devil in the details, or patron saint of the unholy. Let's say "vampire," if you require the comfort of a familiar word. Resurrected, transformed, here for the long haul – I am Alexios, and this is my manifesto, my sacred text, my two goddamned cents' worth. For seven thousand years I've passed like a scalpel through skin from one era to the next and drifted like smoke from place to place. I've seen it all, life and death and everything in between, more than once, so I can say with confidence that I've earned the right to speak my mind straight-up and unvarnished, taking no prisoners and telling it like it is. No one is safe from my scrutiny, nothing is sacred, and there is no sanctuary...not in the loneliest corners of your mind nor in the dreariest shadows of your heart. *Haud sileo. Haud pacis.* I won't lie, but neither will I be presumptuous enough to claim that I tell the truth. How about a bracing slap in the face with reality instead?

What is truth? It seems like only yesterday that I whispered the deceptively simple question in Pontius Pilate's ear, and little did I know I would ignite a debate that would blister through the centuries as historians and holy men, philosophers and poets argue and debate to no end over the meaning hiding behind those three short, sharp words. I've posed the question to many – to the good, the bad, and the indifferent – but I've never gotten an answer from anyone. Hitler just stared at me with bleary-eyed confusion in the stifling cocoon of his bunker before he pulled the trigger on that spring day. As his final moments faded away, Cardinal Richelieu couldn't comprehend a truth that would snuff out his magnificent life, and even the "Messiah" himself remained silent. You see, it's a trick question; there is no answer, there is no truth. There's only a sad collection of realities. "Truth" suggests something profound, or at least substantial, but "reality" simply is. That's life. People try to polish it and dress it up as something imbued with hope, something that won't crush their spirit, but life is not a bowl of cherries or a walk in the park. Life isn't a cabaret, old chum, it's a nut-house, a fucking asylum people spend their every waking moment desperately trying to escape from, but there's only one way out, and it isn't an exit stage left or a sweet chariot comin' for to carry you home...and *that's* the truth. I've never denied reality; I've always accepted it, looked it straight in the eye, so now I'm ready to share it, to put reality on display like a piece of fine art or a strange insect preserved under glass.

Here's reality for you: last night I went to Home Depot to buy a bag of potting soil for a few houseplants I neglected well past the point of benefitting from the therapeutic properties of clean, fresh dirt when I noticed a man with a stroller attempting to attract my attention. He would look directly at me, smile broadly, and nod his head crisply in a manner that made matters instantly clear that his intentions were not unseemly. Then he would direct my gaze downward to the dreadful, squirming, dimple-cheeked fat larva strapped into the blue and yellow padded seat of the stroller. Clearly I was expected to respond with a beaming rapturous smile aimed in admiration at his kicking, arm-twirling, blank-faced infant. But rather, I offered him a knowing smirk, then turned and left the store leaving the young father to wither like one of my parched philodendrons. The man quickly aimed his smile elsewhere, but his eyes gave him away; his eyes told the real story. His eyes showed the misery, the unhappiness, the quiet panic he tried with considerable but futile effort to banish from his mind.

Reality.

That man wanted to be anywhere but standing in a glorified hardware store with a drooling baby in a stroller. He knew that the hopes and aspirations for the life he had always dreamed of would fade away more and more with baby's first-step, with every birthday, with each school play and little league game until he disappeared completely, right along with his dreams. So he smiled at his fellow shoppers, hoping no one would notice his eyes screaming out in pain and tortured resignation. He battles reality, he holds it at bay and masks it with the suffocating obligation of fatherly pride. Cynical? A bleak, jaundiced point of view? Perhaps. Perhaps you were expecting—probably hoping—a vampire's take on things both large and small would be different. Maybe you wanted a manufactured monster, bats and buckets of blood or brocaded weariness sighing and heaving under the ponderous weight of an overripe Victorian eternity. Find your fantasies elsewhere; I'm not here to amuse you or indulge you, but I will take you by the hand and walk you through the wreckage of life, across a desolate landscape strewn with the debris of desperation and bitter disappointment. I'll point out all that you strive to turn away from and tell you everything you don't want to hear. You might not like what I have to say, and my words may unsettle you, but trust me, my vision of the world— and of you— is crystal clear.

—*Alexios*

QUINTESSENCE

MARTYRS

Martyrs are venerated above all other saints. Piety and a talent for a few convincing magic tricks or a familiar manner with animals pale in comparison to an agonizing execution carried out before a cheering mob of heathen spectators. During the formative years of Christianity, when the first wave of martyrs spilled their holy blood under the persecutions of Nero and Domitian, I personally witnessed several of the gory extravaganzas that fast-tracked victims to certain beatification. After the fact, the narratives were molded, the stories polished and perfected. Mythologies were carefully created around the blessedly deceased that bore little resemblance to the grimy events I watched unfold in ancient cities like Rome and Alexandria. According to the fictionalized accounts, those sacrificed saints accepted their ghastly finales with serene reserve and occasionally a glib parting remark. But faith folds before the torment of the flesh, and I recall that a good deal of shrieking and screaming and gasping and pleading accompanied the martyrdoms I was present for. Involuntary physical response doesn't carry the same élan as spiritual repose, so more suitable fables were needed to enrapture the flock of true believers, and to this very day the heavenly fellowship of martyrs is still revered for facing beheadings, bludgeonings, roastings, dismemberments, stonings, scaldings, crucifixions, and hails of arrows with dignity.

There is nothing dignified about the process of either birth or death, and the tawdry circus that plays out between those two competing milestones is far more ignoble than glorious, even in the most charmed circumstances. Long ago I determined that dignity was a myth, a construct created to make people feel better about their shabby lives, and often just an elevated term for slack-jawed indifference. No one is ever coronated, elected, or enthroned with dignity, and certainly, no one ever wins an Oscar, hits the jackpot, or claims a gold medal with grace. Power, success, and fame might periodically require a performance art piece of well-heeled reserve, but no one bullies their way to the front of the line or battles all the way up to the top perch with any amount of decorum. The inauguration of America's Commander-in-Chief is a spectacle carried out with as much dignity as a Super Bowl halftime show. The president takes the oath of office with the usual suspects of holy men and politicians on hand, along with insufferable poets and pop stars as opening acts for the bloated main event. Even the most powerful man in the world can quickly fall back to Earth thanks to a seemingly innocent but undignified tradition, and as the president makes his way from one inaugural gala to the next, he's required to take the customary first dance alone on stage with the First Lady at each glamorous ball. Clumsily swaying back and forth while clinging to each other like the last survivors on a sinking life raft, the presidential couple dances with queasy discomfort while a singer chosen for a lack of high-profile behavioral problems rather than a remarkable singing voice screeches out a nearly unrecognizable version of an R&B standard or Beatles song. Dignity?

If dignity truly existed, there would be no tramp stamps or all-you-can-eat restaurants, no one would ever speak in public or engage in sexual activity. And it's the complete absence of dignity that ensured successful careers for Cleopatra and Shelley Winters. Dignity is a crumb thrown to the unfortunate. People suffer with dignity, they face adversity with dignity; they endure broken hearts, financial ruin, and death with dignity only because they've grown exhausted from whining and casting blame for their trials and tribulations. A dignified comportment hides the embarrassment of failure or wards off the crippling panic of despair when life's cruelty wraps around you like a constrictor's death embrace.

My modest artistic ability doesn't extend to a presumption that I'm capable of producing any meaningful work myself, but last week I participated in a life drawing class at the request of an acquaintance who was making his debut as a figure model. Jon claimed that he sought out the modeling assignment as a way to earn some extra money for a trip he was planning to Europe, although his full-time job is a well-compensated position with a large financial firm, so I suspected his real motives were somewhat more intimate. Not strikingly attractive like a Brazilian fashion model, but instead blandly handsome like a catalog model, Jon is remarkably well-built and exceedingly aware of his attributes; however, when his equally fetching long-time partner, Eric, unceremoniously dumped him for a twenty-six-year-old rugby-playing bartender, Jon reacted in a way that could never be characterized as "dignified." Forty-three years old, humiliated and angry, Jon lashed out, and our unlikely friendship was forged by his need for an ever-expanding audience that would patiently listen to the vindictive tirades he aimed at the wayward Eric. Before long, complaining wasn't enough to keep Jon satisfied, especially since his former spouse was publicly quite thrilled with the new situation, so Jon began to seek attention – anything that would validate his desirability. He needed to convince himself, and everyone else, that he was still a valued commodity, still very much in the game.

"The regulars bring their own supplies, but I can set you up with some paper and charcoal for tonight," Celeste, the life drawing class instructor, told me with a smile as she led me to an easel holding a large pad of newsprint and a small dish filled with charcoal sticks of various sizes. "That's everything you need," she smiled again, but floating beneath her amicable exterior was the prickly message that next time, I'd better show up equipped and ready to go. "I've been teaching this class for nearly fifteen years. It's very casual, and my students are a mixed bag, from advanced to beginners. Everyone works at their own comfort level here…I don't want anyone to feel intimidated," she said, instantly making me feel self-conscious. "Have you done much drawing?" She asked it in the same way a doctor would adopt an innocent tone of voice to inquire whether or not a patient routinely indulged in some unsavory personal habit. "Just doodled over the years," I answered without confessing to the specifics that I had used a stick to scratch out my first little drawing in the sand when I was a small boy several millennia before Alexander conquered the known world. "Great!" Celeste chirped, then abruptly turned and headed off to welcome a few of her favored regulars who I assumed to be the advanced students. The studio was quiet; no one socialized or exchanged bits and pieces of friendly conversation. Everyone was seated at their easels in silent introspection waiting for the class to begin, then Celeste looked up at the clock and said, "Okay, guys, let's get started tonight," in a smoker's voice that sounded ironically similar to the elderly watercolor instructress in the COPD inhaler commercial I saw while watching a program on Animal Planet about exotic pets who kill their owners. "Our model this evening is Jon," she announced, and the class commenced.

Jon walked in wearing a white robe with thin blue stripes to no fanfare or applause, then stepped up onto a wooden pallet at the front of the studio, opened his robe, and shed it like Diana Ross flinging off her ermine cape after making a grand entrance in one of her elaborately-staged and costumed concerts. But once exposed, Jon's demeanor changed. No "oohs" or "aahhhs" acknowledged his undraped appearance, no collective gasp of admiration rose up from the students who merely regarded him with the same impassive scrutiny that greeted the heavyset older woman who had posed for them the week before. Jon froze, naked and alone, and he suddenly realized with damning lucidity where he was—and, more importantly, why. "First pose," Celeste said softly as if she were in a church or library, but Jon barely moved. With arms hanging down, he tried to lift his hands upward. His eyes closed, and his head fell back slightly to one side…and I began to sketch.

My style in general has never been complicated or overly fussy, and with nothing more than a few clean, crisp swipes of my charcoal stick, I had committed Jon's anguish to a sheet of newsprint with alarming accuracy. While the other students blended and shaded, I took a few moments to add some arrows to my composition until Jon's likeness was transformed into the pierced image of the martyred St. Sebastian. "New position," Celeste intoned in a murmur, and Jon shifted uncomfortably from foot to foot, then swiveled himself around as I turned my attention elsewhere. The studio was silent save for the delicate, muffled scratching of charcoal on paper, and in that quiet, hushed sound I heard the stories of the people working around me. I sketched a woman who sat at an easel on the far side of the room. She came to class every Thursday night to escape for just a brief time from her shrill, demanding teenage daughter and dour, surly son. Once a week she found a respite from attending to her husband's needs as if she were his personal valet. Her drawing looked nothing like Jon, nor was it even recognizably human. It was a hazy blur of shapes without personality, without an identity...she was drawing herself. "Change pose," Celeste instructed like the ringmaster in this sideshow of damaged souls. An old gentleman in corduroy pants and a navy blue sweater focused on one aspect of Jon and rendered it with a dazzlingly intricate realism that faded away to an elegantly smoky tangle of feather-soft smudges on his finely textured, pristine white paper. The class allowed him to sit down at an easel with a sharpened pencil and to set his exquisite natural talent free – the talent that lay hidden below layers of a life he never aspired to after his parents had smothered and stamped out the ember of his dreams many decades earlier when they dismissed his artistry as silly and useless. With each new pose, each change of position, I rendered another of the students taking flight from the grinding, dull torment of their lives...at least for a brief 90 minutes. They were martyrs, each in their own way, who would never be sanctified or exalted or immortalized in fables, paintings, and feast days. They suffered in silence as the ponderous weight of simply moving from one day to the next crushed the life out them.

I waited for Jon to get dressed, then we left the studio and made our way out into the cold night. As we stood in front of his building, he glanced down to the sidewalk and asked, "So, how did I do...you know, how was I?" "Dignified," I replied, and without looking at me, he nodded his head, turned, and went inside. We haven't spoken since.

A COLD NOVEMBER NIGHT, 1963

America grieved. All of its quarreling factions, its patchwork of regions, united from the coast on one ocean to the coast on another. The entire nation fused together, became one in its pain, and mourned its loss. I looked down at the stack of papers on the damp sidewalk, picked one up, and paid the attendant at the newsstand. "Hard to believe, isn't it?" the man asked, taking the coins from my outstretched hand. "Certainly is," I answered back as I walked away and watched the sad-eyed people moving past me, hushed and quiet, through the cold November night. A bus pulled up to the curb, shuddered to a stop, and the doors opened with a creaking squeal. I stepped on, found myself a seat next to a window, and unfolded the newspaper. *Assassination.* The word hung in the buzzing, sickly glow of the lights that cast a dull, yellow-gray haze on my fellow passengers, and that word seemed to follow close behind everyone walking down the street. It crept up beside people waiting for a green light that would allow them to make their way safely from corner to corner, and it kept pace with the cars that seemed to move in slow motion. The assassination had shocked the nation, shocked the world, and left me to ponder how the alarming event fit into my intricate puzzle. In the years since my masterpiece ended with Soviet trucks rumbling through the ruins of Berlin and Emperor Hirohito's surrender crackling over the radio, I'd been busy prodding the paranoia and stoking the fears of an anxious and unsettled world until the Cold War had unleashed a nightmare of international malice, institutional perfidy, and dangerous personal impulse. The shots that rang out on that Friday morning in Dallas, the shots that reverberated around the world, were hatched in the nest of unrest I had carefully created. The photograph on the front page of my newspaper—stark, crisp black and white—looked artfully artificial. Jack Ruby with his dark suit and gun was like something from a gangster movie. Detective Jim Leavelle stepping back in stunned amazement, and Lee Harvey Oswald captured in the moment when history claimed him – it all appeared posed, staged, oddly theatrical, but it was real. I opened the paper, and inside was a grainy picture of the president and his wife in the open-top car, the morning sun shining on their smiling faces just minutes before the end.

The nation lamented the loss of neither a president nor a man, but a symbol...a symbol elastic and pliable enough to fit a country's general need as well as each citizen's specific desire. Whether terrifying or enthralling, threatening or comforting, symbols maintain order, keep the unruly masses in line, and set the boundaries that imprison societies searching for a scrap of meaning in the confusion. The hammer and sickle, the Star of David, the Golden Arches, and the double-headed Habsburg eagle...they're all symbols separated by perspective and self-serving agendas, and when a symbol crashes to the ground, a new order is ushered in, a new structure rises up, holding aloft a new symbol that changes the rules of the game. I always work on an epic scale with my schemes and projects built in huge proportions too big for individuals, too big for faces. An instigator-turned-observer once the wheels are set in motion with no need or desire to stain my own hands with the messy end of upheaval and unrest, I only consider the majestically terrible concepts, the shifting lines on the map, the rise and fall of symbols. The terrified faces were just a backdrop as the mighty Babylon was sacked. Standing in the sweaty, reeking Parisian mob, I watched with little regard as dispirited victims were led frightened and confused to the guillotine to die for somebody's cause – maybe the nation's... maybe no one's. The frightened and filthy men crawling through the muddy, bloody trenches of Verdun and the Somme were just colorless, grimy shapes playing out their assigned roles, not sons and brothers and fathers. The bright flashes over Hiroshima and Nagasaki were brilliant symbols of man's capacity to usher in his own extinction, not mosaics of faces. I looked at the president and his wife smiling in the Dallas morning sun, then closed the paper. "Symbols," I whispered, and I pushed aside the memory of a morning sun shining on my own smiling face a very, very long time ago.

The traffic slowly inched past the bus, and my face, a ghostly reflection on the window, floated over the grim, dark evening. The bus wheezed, lurched slightly, and stopped. A handful of silent, sullen people boarded. "Excuse me, is this seat taken?" I turned and saw a woman standing in the aisle. She was middle-aged, neatly dressed in blandly styled clothes, and she possessed the type of pleasantness that rendered her instantly forgettable. "No," I said, "please sit down." "Thank you," she said flatly, then she loosened her scarf, pulled at the hem of her coat, and shifted in the seat until she had found a comfortable position. I sat still, not breathing, then drew in a breath. I can tell much about a person by her scent, and the woman smelled of sweet dusting powder, probably a gift for Mother's Day, or perhaps for her birthday, purchased by her husband at a modest department store like Sears or J.C. Penney. She was grateful for the expression of affection, but it wasn't what she had really wanted, and she felt a pang of guilt whenever she thought of nicer, more pleasing choices her husband could have wrapped up and hidden away until surprising her on that special day, so every morning she dutifully dusted herself lightly with the powder. She had stopped on her way home to pick up a few things for dinner and jostled the brown paper shopping bag of groceries on her lap. A small bunch of colorful flowers poked out of the bag. "I thought they might cheer things up a little," the woman said. She looked at the newspaper in my lap. "Like a bad dream, a nightmare, I can't believe it's really happening," she said sadly. I nodded. "My husband says it was Castro or the mob, but I don't think so," the woman said, shaking her head, "because he was Catholic, that's what I think." I smoothed the paper with my pale hand and turned to the woman. "One man's finger on a trigger, that's all it was." "But…I mean," and the woman turned in her seat towards me, "that makes it sound so simple. There must be more to it than just…*him.*" She pointed contemptuously to the picture of Oswald doubled over in mortal pain. "Sometimes things really are just simple," I smiled. "Most people can't comprehend simple. People can understand simple-minded all too well, but true simplicity – the purity of it – is hard for many to absorb and process." I folded my paper and said, "People like to ornament everything with convoluted meaning and hidden motives…to avoid coming face-to-face with the truth, I suppose. It's easier to lose yourself in the complicated than it is to acknowledge the frightening face of simple, primitive reality." The woman studied my sharp, inscrutable features for a moment, and then sighed, "You might be right."

"I remember during the war…you're too young to remember

it like I do," she said to the ancient vampire sharing her seat on the bus, "I thought the world was ending. My parents kept telling me to be strong, be strong and we'd survive it. We survived even though my brother never came back," she said with a smile that quickly faded, "but everything changed. Things are probably better in many ways now...but the world just seems meaner, colder." She lifted her shopping bag slightly and set it back down on her lap. "And now this...things won't be the same after this." "The world doesn't stand still," I laughed. "It constantly shifts and changes and reinvents itself; otherwise, everything would just stop." "But does it always have to be so hard?" the woman asked wearily. My genuine expression of astonishment was apparent. I've never been able to understand why people can't see things as I do, to view the world with my same unforgiving certainty. "Yes! It's always hard. It's never easy. Oh, people like to cling to their fantasies about...well...look at those flowers," I said, pointing to the small bouquet in the brown paper bag. "You probably think flowers are beautiful and delicate, but in fact they grow by sinking their roots in soil, and what is that but a pile of rotting dead matter?" The woman looked down at her flowers as I continued. "And people see a bud open and think that it's a gentle, fragile, lovely act, but it's really quite savage. That bud," I said pointing to the flowers again, "tears itself apart. It rips itself open and stretches itself in a ghastly, horrific way, petal by petal, until it turns itself completely inside out...but all people see is a pretty blossom." The woman looked at me, speechless. "The whole world is like that," I said. "A civilization must crack and splinter and fall to pieces before another can emerge and rise up higher – rise up and bloom on the ruins of what came before, sinking its roots in the death of dreams and the decay of spent lives." I looked at the woman and frowned slightly. "Do you see what I mean?" I unfolded my newspaper again and swept my hand across the history playing out on the front page. "Yes, things will be different after this, that's the way the world works. From destruction comes creation." The woman stared out of the bus window at the dark night passing by and said, "I wish it didn't have to be that way." "A wish is just the empty shell of hope," I said. The bus came to a stop. "Oh!" The woman suddenly cried. "Oh! My stop!" She stood up quickly and collected herself. "It was nice to meet you," she said as she turned and hurried towards the door. I noticed the woman's small bunch of flowers lying on the empty seat next to me. "Excuse me," I called out to her, "you dropped your flowers." She turned and smiled as she stepped out of the door. "You can keep them. Maybe they'll cheer things up a little."

REAL LIFE, REAL DEATH

"All the world's a stage,
And all the men and women merely players..."
– William Shakespeare

Coaches may inspire, prophets may captivate, and politicians may charm, but every last one of them brainwashes their gullible followers with carefully manufactured mumbo jumbo designed to explain it all in convoluted yet consumer-friendly bite-sized morsels. Bullshit. The universal predicament can be summed up in simple, straightforward terms: life is a big show — for a few it's Broadway, while for most it's dinner theater, and unfortunately for others it's a seedy strip club with a sticky floor. No one makes a move – right or wrong, good or bad, noble or not – that isn't a carefully conceived act, performance art presented with earnest insincerity. "And all the men and women merely players," right to the end...

"Do you think the casket will be open?" I asked as Richard waved his arm to flag a cab. "I don't see how it could be, considering what happened," he said, opening the taxi door with a loud squawking creak, "but morticians can do amazing things these days…you know, almost like special effects make-up." Our driver, Rakhshan, angrily sounded his horn at a woman who looked like she was prepared to dart across the street before he could pull away from the curb, and with that hostile fanfare, we headed off to the memorial service for a man who died in a car crash that brought rush hour traffic to a complete standstill for several hours. A fire engine, three ambulances, two tow trucks, and a splashy show of squad cars were on hand when Richard's friend Ken was pulled from the twisted wreckage that ended his Monday evening commute home, his plans to watch a television show about lawyers who win every case…and his life. I was surprised when my neighbor asked me to accompany him to the service; we've only ever spoken in a casual manner, but I nonetheless appreciated the grim invitation. "Thanks for coming," Richard said, "I hate walking into things like this alone. I won't know anyone there, besides…well, Ken."

The chapel hosting Ken's send-off was decorated in appropriately masculine shades of deep colonial blue, while across the hall a dusty rose-colored viewing room was occupied by an elderly woman who died after losing her long battle with stomach cancer. Although impeccably staged to avoid even the slightest suggestion of bad taste, a whisper of vulgarity clung to every chintz jabot, marble-topped table, and velvet upholstered chair in the funeral home. "Closed," Richard said with noticeable disappointment. "The casket is closed," he repeated with embellishment to his initial single-word observation, in case I might have missed the obvious when we walked into the crowded, flower-filled room.

We took two seats in the last row of chairs just in time for the service to begin. A minister invited by Ken's parents stepped up to a dark mahogany lectern, smiled uncomfortably, and launched into an awkwardly impersonal eulogy for a man he had never met. The reverend spouted a few boilerplate slogans about "those left behind" and angels carrying Ken off to a better place, but the heavy lifting had been done by two firemen who wrenched Ken's broken body from his twisted Honda, and the only thing left behind was the wrecked car for the tow trucks to haul away. The man of God ended his brief tribute with a murky reference to finding meaning in the meaningless, and I assumed the service had come to a quick conclusion when Ken's mother stood, tugged down her black blazer, and took the reverend's place at the podium.

She paused to wipe tears away with a wadded-up tissue, then announced, "I am Kenny's mom," like a recovering drunk introducing herself at an A.A. mixer. Kenny's mom laughed and sobbed simultaneously in a way you would normally only see in a Lifetime Channel movie as she told a heartwarming tale of her son's childhood. Next up was Kenny's dad, followed by Kenny's sister; both shared their own recollections from Ken's younger years. The deceased man was never mentioned by his grieving family. They all spoke of their son and brother in the idealized terms of a childhood filtered through a haze of *Leave It to Beaver* fictionalized perfection. Several of Ken's friends took turns speaking fondly of the dead, but in their stories of memorable celebrations and events, I found nothing personal or profound about the man who died in a ghastly accident just three blocks from the sanctuary of his home. I discovered more about the eulogizers than the eulogized and was left with a vivid picture of a loving mother, a good father, and supportive friends, but none of their words painted a portrait of the man in the closed casket. His reality remained a mystery. "All the world's a stage…" and everybody wants to be in the spotlight. As I listened to the cast of mourners, Ken seemed to be a supporting player in each of their personal theatrical productions. "Are you going to speak?" I leaned over and whispered discretely to Richard, but he reacted with surprise, frowned slightly, and said, "Me?! No...no...we just hooked up online a few times. I didn't know him that well."

There is a moment right before night begins its surrender to morning when a stillness settles over everything, and in that moment of true darkness, I returned to the funeral home, unseen like a misty shadow, a fog rolling in off of a troubled ocean. Commonplace curiosity, not the fleeting rush of forbidden excitement, had gotten the best of me, and in the gloomy, empty chapel I stood alone in front of Ken's casket studying the smiling sphinx captured in a vacation snapshot enlarged to fit an 8×10 frame. The real Ken lay hidden beneath the bronze coffin lid buffed to a showroom luster, and without hesitation I opened it. Nothing. The silk-lined box contained no answer, no hint of insight, no suggestion of the man Ken had been in life. With lopsided arms crossed over its chest, the dead man's body was arranged in an approximation of symmetry, dressed up in a blue and purple striped sport shirt that would have looked good paired with either jeans or a nice dress pant, but it seemed hardly the subdued and formal attire typically chosen to send a person off to the Great Hereafter. The undertaker had attempted to recreate Ken's face and head as a waxy work of art with strangely exaggerated features, and the thankless effort was shellacked with heavy vaudeville-like makeup and topped with a synthetic wig. A life-sized ventriloquist's dummy slumbered in eternal repose...not the man who had until recently worried about bills or laughed with friends or wondered what the next day might bring. Maybe the remnants of Ken's head were scooped up into a container and later discretely tucked away in the lower regions of the coffin, or maybe Streets and Sanitation workers hosed the gory bits and pieces of bone and tooth and tissue off the pavement and into the sewer. For all practical purposes, Ken had disappeared. The reality of the man vanished in the final mangled moments of his life. "All the world's a stage, and all the men and women merely players." It's all a goddamn act, everything is, and maybe the reality of a person, the true essence of who they fundamentally are, is too personal to put on public display, so it remains protected, hidden from view, and then it evaporates along with the last dying breath. As I slipped out of the funeral home, a sudden movement took me by surprise – my own reflection in a huge mirror with a heavy, ornately gilded frame. Unlike fictional vampires in novels and movies and folklore, I'm not shielded from the certainty of my own reflected image, and taken off-guard, unprepared, removed from the carefully managed presentation that I send out onto life's stage, I was startled to see such a pensive face staring out from the silvery surface of the looking glass instead of the austere monster's mask.

Up one street and down another, a turn here and another there...I followed a path home that took me past the spot where Ken met his end. Stores were closed, people slept behind their darkened apartment windows, and even the flowers in the big planters on each corner looked as if they dozed in the final moments of the night. A dead rat lay tucked against the curb; its body was flattened and compressed into a nearly unrecognizable shape. Judging by the carcass' appearance, I guessed the rodent had been dead for several days. Perhaps it died on the same corner on the same day as Ken. No one eulogized the rat. No one expressed their grief over its passing or recalled personal memories of special moments they shared with the dearly departed vermin. Thousands of cars must have rolled over the smashed animal, and countless people stepped around it on their way to work, on their way back home, or on their way to somewhere that would salve the sting of life for a minute or two. No one stopped to consider the terror the rat felt when it realized that its dash across the street would end under the wheel of a bus, or of the joy it experienced on a better day when it found a slimy scrap of someone's lunch that had fallen into the gutter, but still, the crushed little rat's presence leached its way into the minds of everyone who passed by. It was a sad and silent reminder that in the end there is nothing...no kingdom come, no joyous reunions, no paradise, no peace. A sharp burning sensation that left a frigid, lingering chill washed over my face and arms. The first blush of dawn began to spread a sickly pink glow over the sky.

I arrived back home and settled in for my sleep, and as I drifted off, I thought of Ken's picture set in tribute on his casket. He looked happy in the tropical sunlight of some popular vacation destination, but whether he smiled because he was genuinely content or just relieved to be away from work, his frozen city, or his everyday life for a brief time, I couldn't tell. He was nice-looking in a non-threatening "regular guy" sort of way, but his image quickly began to fade from my mind, and all I was left with were the bright colors of the photo. "You can't take it with you," the old saying goes, but I truly believe you do.

HERE TODAY, GONE TOMORROW

I've been away, gone, AWOL, hiding out, undetectable, secreted off to an undisclosed location, POOF!—vanished without a trace. Here today, gone tomorrow. Although I'm tempted to embellish my absence and say that I've been busy stirring up cultural resentments, poisoning the well of political discourse and fanning the flames of international discontent, I must admit that I nodded off while watching an overwrought melodramatic TV series that follows the exploits of Chicago firefighters and woke up several months later to find the stalwart Bear Grylls gracing my television screen as he scolded and cajoled an odd assortment of attention seekers through the rigors of wilderness survival. Bear must certainly know that no one escapes this mess in living-breathing condition, but nonetheless, he urged his ragtag teams of whining fiancés, dumpy middle-aged married couples, muscle-bound homosexuals, and parent/child combos to believe that there is something profound waiting for them on top of the peak or that rappelling to the bottom of a gorge is a worthwhile spiritual endeavor. It's all horseshit, and Bear Grylls – like everyone else – is running and climbing and jumping away from the terrifying truth that there's nothing either up there or down there but the eventual end. Mr. Grylls compels his charges onward and promises the mountain will give them strength, but once they've crested the summit, they all look exhausted and fitfully anxious as they stare off into the nothingness.

Time is the most beguiling of commodities, coveted and squandered in equal measure. People pine for the "good old days," or fret, "If only I had more time," or long to go back and start it all over again, yet every Monday morning people count the minutes to Friday, wishing away a week's worth of life for a couple of days that will undoubtedly be a disappointment. For me, time isn't a curse, but rather an organizational tool to keep my eternity in reasonably tidy order. I don't want to simply wander the world aimlessly forever, and I'm too damn vain to lose track of my impressive accomplishments in a haze of lazy forgetfulness, but a limitless supply of time can take its toll on even a hearty immortal creature like me, and sometimes I am overcome by the ennui of it all and choose to exercise the luxury I possess to close my eyes for a few months, years, or decades until I wake up refreshed and with a renewed vigor to stare down the mighty crush of existence with my pitch black eyes.

I'm bored.

Oh, sure, these are indeed compelling times. Technological advancements are racing forward at the speed of light, and now even very young children are computer savvy little beasts who can boast an impressive list of beloved bookmarked porn websites. The auto industry is swiftly redefining itself for a new age, and the current crop of 3-D movies is filled with high-definition marvels – no longer a murky blur of green and red confusion. Just about anyone can record a dance pop hit in the comfort of their own home with a bossa nova techno beat only a click away on their laptop or become a momentary sensation courtesy a self-produced YouTube clip, but the bigger picture has lost its vibrancy. The colors have bled, the hues have faded. Events that marched forward as I napped all seemed weighted down by a dull familiarity. Cops and crooks traded bullets and blame, and the expected spate of protest marches and televised looting that sprang up in various ghettos like packaged, seamless, corporately sponsored events were lackluster affairs, and the outrage seemed forced and artificial as everyone impatiently waited for their moment of offense and outrage before the cable news cameras... been there, done that before. Egypt was mired in a constant state of disruption over various imposed or self-inflicted iron-fisted regimes, but ironically, my most vivid personal memories of the Egyptian people go all the way back to their Golden Age when I watched them politely toil under centuries of divine despots who claimed to be Ra's viceroys on Earth. Everything old is new again. Democrats battle Republicans in the ongoing vaudeville of political one-upmanship that has caused the Great Experiment of Democracy to fall further into a paralyzing stagnation. Politicians texted and tweeted their manliness; unwashed pop stars twerked and tweaked...the same old story. It was the best of times, it was the most tedious of times. Someone woke up grumpy...perhaps I should have slept a while longer.

Once I had shaken the post-nap malaise, I decided my first order of business was to head off to the drug store to buy a package of light bulbs and a hairstyling product I saw advertised in a men's fashion magazine. I expected a quick trip in and out of the store, but a large woman wearing sensible shoes who looked to be around fifty-five stepped in front of me as I approached the checkout line and then proceeded to pay for her purchase with a personal check. My annoyance faded when I spied the illustration of a child angel with puffy wings that appeared utterly useless for flight, golden curls surrounding her round face and a white shimmering nightgown on the front of the check. Bathed in rays of a heavenly light so gentle it would never scorch her tender, pink-cheeked skin even in the absence of a high quality sunblock, the little girl angel sputtered, stalled, and jammed the cash register's printer until with great effort the contraption expelled a sadly crumpled cherub. Ignoring the grinding and clattering protest emanating from the small plastic box, the woman slipped her light blue pen into a slot in her checkbook and closed it to reveal a cover with bulbous mounds of painted clouds that looked like pastel blue and white cotton candy emblazoned with the slogan, "I Believe in Angels" in a floridly scripted font. People declare their belief in God and country, angels, love at first sight, and that life is fair. You cling to a belief that everything will work out in the end and that a reality TV star cares that you follow him on Twitter. The public show of belief masks the private admission that it's all bullshit. I was about to ask the woman why she chose to believe in angels instead of UFOs, the living Elvis, or undead vampires, but she lumbered away, paused to check her receipt, then walked through the hissing automatic doors to fade away into the night. *Back to where?* I wondered. *Back to what?* "Will that be all for you tonight?" the cashier, a young man who looked vaguely like a skinnier Ryan Seacrest, asked. "Oh," I said. I turned away from the doors and absentmindedly picked up a small, potted, grafted cactus that was sitting in a cardboard display next to the register and added it to my purchase.

My unplanned nap caused me to miss the heroics and romances of fictional TV fire fighters, but a real-life fireman drama unfolded last night on the corner of my block. I walked up as two fire engines, an ambulance, and several squad cars with their sirens howling and their lights flashing stopped in front of a modest apartment building situated ironically next to a stately vintage courtyard condominium. "Someone in the building smelled a dead body!" a woman walking her hyperactive Boston bulldog told me with breathless excitement after I had joined the crowd of neighborhood gawkers. Narrowing my eyes, I scanned the scene suspiciously and drew in a breath. I smelled something bad. The faint odor of decay wafted in the air, but it wasn't death.

Death. People assume that my peculiar personal history causes me to view death through an enchanted midnight blue lens, or that my very existence veneers death with velvety dark glamor. Death is a momentary event; only the details surrounding it, the environment that hosts it, the players that set it in motion add character to the fleeting few seconds of the end. There was nothing glamorous about my own death. The mechanics, if not the circumstances, were quite ordinary. I remember struggling futilely to grip even a fading ember of life in those fateful final moments before everything suddenly went black. When I rose from the darkness and opened my eyes, I saw with crystal clarity that death is not noble and that life is simply a ravenous, savagely mindless force. Over these countless centuries, I've smelled death in the pass of Thermopylae, in the Teutoburg Forest, in Gettysburg and Leningrad. I've smelled it under dark, dirty expressway underpasses and in hospitals, nursing homes, and refrigerated, perfumed funeral parlors. The noxious scent that reached me on the street wasn't the stench of the end, but of hopelessness and despair.

Slowly, I worked my way through the crowd until I reached one of the firemen standing on the sidewalk. He wiped a sleeve across his face, waved his hand towards the apartment building's glass doors, and said to a cop waiting for information, "It's real bad in there." "Dead?" the policeman asked. "No, she's alive," the firefighter said, putting the back of his hand to his lips. "She's fine…I mean, she seems like she's okay, but it's…gross…you know…her apartment…really bad in there." Medics appeared in the building's lobby with a woman they had wrapped in a crisp, white sheet that was bunched high around her shoulders. A personal hell exploded into a public horror, and word of the filth and squalor that she had been living in spread like a disease through the crowd. Stunned silence was broken by a few giggles and gags from people, both neighbors and strangers alike. The woman was led through the parted crowd like Blanche Dubois throwing herself on the "kindness of strangers," and in one last desperate effort to regain even a sliver of dignity, she tried to smooth the crumpled sheet around her chin. I recognized her. She was the woman with the angel checkbook I had seen in the drugstore. The ambulance doors closed, and the woman disappeared in a scream of sirens off to the psych ward of a nearby hospital where someone would sort through the wreck of her life. Here today, gone tomorrow.

I wonder when the woman who lived in filth began to believe in angels. Did her belief rise higher as she sank lower in a sewer of despair? Did she believe that someday she would find peace in pristine, powder-soft clouds bathed in clean, radiant white light, or did she desperately need to believe that something existed somewhere that was better than this rotten world? I made my way through the chattering onlookers, across the street, and back home. I turned on the TV just in time to see Bear Grylls rub his hands together, pat his knees, and say, "This was a hard decision." The remaining teams of survivalists exchanged nervous glances in the flickering light of the campfire. Then, with noticeable compassion, Bear told an exhausted, overweight married couple, "I'm sorry, you'd never get out alive." Here today, gone tomorrow.

CRAZY

It only takes a moment.

This old world is a crazy place, and it has been ever since the first brute to stand erect on two legs bashed his buddy's brains out with a rock. But it's the crazy people who make things happen for better or for worse, who reach for that impossible high note or gaze up at the stars and see something more than diamonds sparkling on black velvet…or who set the whole fucking place on fire. The popular notion of crazy is based on the number of bodies a person has buried in his yard or the tally of victims he racks up in the name of God or Country, but crazy takes on countless shapes and guises, from the harmlessly eccentric to the criminally insane. That lovely painting of a starry night wouldn't hang on a museum wall if van Gogh hadn't been mentally disturbed, and if Francis Ford Coppola hadn't lost his mind in the hot, humid jungles of the Philippines, there would be no *Apocalypse Now*. Capote's madness produced a ground-breaking masterpiece, while Hitler and his goons exhaled a lunacy that infected an entire goddamn nation. Life incessantly chasing after you like a drooling, slobbering, snapping, rabid dog is enough to drive anyone crazy, and some people can take that shit and mold it into a thing of beauty, but others, possessing a very different type of talent, bend and stretch it into something unspeakable. To be honest, I'm surprised my own mental composure has remained so remarkably even-keeled over these past thousands and thousands of years, but I've always understood insanity, and I appreciate the usefulness of it in others. When I review my resume and contemplate the wars I've instigated, the turmoil I've stirred up, the revolutions I've set in motion, I'll be the first to admit that I owe much of my success to crazy people. If my fearsome feats of historical horror are ever acknowledged, celebrated, and commemorated with a gilded award at a fancy televised red-carpet ceremony, I'll grasp my golden statuette in my cold, dead hands, and with tears welling up in my black eyes, I'll say, "I want to thank all the crazy people. There are too many crazy people...I can't remember their names."

Some names are impossible to forget. The dismal room was barely lit by the dim glow cast from a few nearly spent candles, but even in the sheltering darkness, the old man was a ghastly sight to behold. His skin, a nauseating palette of sickly grays and terminal yellows, was sunken in around his cheekbones and eye sockets like decayed, moldy leather. A large ulcer had opened up on his deeply lined forehead, and another sore ran with a viscous fluid from the crease beside his nose. He picked at a huge, blackened scab just below his bottom lip with a ragged, discolored fingernail and moaned, "I don't want to die this way, to go out like this...history will torment me for eternity." For a moment I thought he was about to weep, but he held his emotions in check and stared with stoic Roman silence into the gloomy blackness of his private chambers. "Oh, your legacy," I said to the dying old Emperor Tiberius. "They'll be brutal, that's for certain, all of them – the historians and gossips and playwrights – no one will have a good thing to say about you. You'll be a villain for the ages," I informed him coldly. "But why should you care? Once you're dead, you won't hear the insults and slander, you won't have a front row seat to witness the spectacle of your filthy secrets dragged out on stage for all to see," I added as a barbed consolation. He rubbed a skeletal hand over a face that had been corrupted and diseased by years of paranoia, cruelty, and perverse lusts. Tiberius wheezed a wet, gurgling sigh and said softly, "Duty, I have a duty."

"What the hell are you talking about?" I asked sharply. "Duty? Duty to the Senate, to the millions of unwashed slobs who hate you? Duty to Rome...to history?" An inspired thought suddenly flashed like fireworks through my mind. I sat down beside the emperor and draped my arm over his skeletal shoulders, "The only duty you have is to leave behind a token of your appreciation...a gift." "A gift?" the puzzled emperor asked, his ravaged features twisted in confusion. "Your nephew...bestow your nephew on Rome as your parting gift," I smiled. "Imagine the possibilities." The very notion seemed to terrify even an old scoundrel like Tiberius. "You can't be suggesting that I should...he's mad!" the emperor gasped in a startled, cracking voice. "Mad? Don't be so polite. He's crazy," I said, then I patted Tiberius on his bony knee and appealed directly to his most paranoid consternations: "Retribution for the unfaithfulness of your most trusted ministers; revenge for the vile gossip spread about you; pure, perfect payback for all the wrongs you've suffered." The emperor clenched his jaw and stared at me, his dying eyes flashing with burning hatred. Then he turned, hung his head, and sobbed. Tears ran down the deep creases on his wrinkled face like streams finding their way to the ocean. The next day, Imperator Tiberius Caesar Augustus amended his will and named the monstrous Caligula as heir to the diadem of Rome.

A select few go malignantly mad like Caligula or become gripped by mad genius like Mozart, but for most people, madness is a lonely affair played out in private, hidden far away from the recognition that confers universal horror or spellbound admiration. History doesn't record it in a messy mix of damning facts and frightening fables. It doesn't grace the most splendid art galleries or become the soundtrack to anyone's life. Most people's madness is confined to their modest homes and the dismal corridors of their tortured minds, but when their dreary little lunacy peeks its head out, the reception it receives is more often than not cruel. A crazy girl recently joined the gym I belong to. I don't know anything about her; she just appeared one day like a damaged package left on a doorstep by the postman, but I'm sure there must be a reason for her oddness. Most likely her mother is to blame, or maybe her fiancé left her for a man. She's thin and wiry and looks like she eats too little and exercises too much, and she walks with tiny, jittery steps while her head swivels loosely around in every direction like it's attached to her neck with a ball and joint mechanism as she searches for something floating in the air between imagination and reality that commands her constantly grinning attention. The other evening I was standing at a rack of dumbbells next to a guy built like Superman who always wears T-shirts with the sleeves and sides cut away, leaving little more than a flap of fabric hanging down his front and another down his back. All of his physique-revealing shredded shirts are printed with some variation of the USMC logo or a Marine Corps inspired slogan, although he's never served in the military himself and has, in fact, worked in the paint department of Sherwin-Williams for the last seven years. The crazy girl stumbled past the superhero paint salesman and me…then she stopped, frowned slightly, and suddenly directed a loud, crisp laugh at us before capering off to an adjoining room. "Fucking crazy chick," the muscular man said to me as he dropped a weight onto the rack. I nodded and agreed that she appeared to be "quite mad." "Fucking insane," he added as a clinical assessment to punctuate his observation. On my way out I saw the crazy girl bent over a workout bench supporting herself on one hand and one knee. She reached around with her free hand rolled into a fist, knocked sharply on her raised behind, and shouted, "There it is! Go! Go! Go!" I wasn't sure what "it" was or where I was being directed to go, so I turned and headed in the opposite direction just to be on the safe side.

"I voted for him...twice," an elderly woman standing on the corner said to me as I passed by. She pointed to a picture of a popular black politician smiling from the window of a newspaper box. "He's colored and all, but he's like Nat King Cole, not like some of these other ones you see on TV or causing hell at the mall." "Is that why you voted for him—because he reminds you of Nat King Cole?" I asked with a measure of morbid fascination. "Well yes," the woman said, then added, "My grandson is an astronaut. He's up there now." She raised her eyes proudly towards the murky night sky – the stars hidden behind a thick layer of street lamp orange haze. A young man wearing a business suit walking several paces in front of me pressed one nostril closed with his finger and discharged a stream of snot onto the sidewalk. He stopped, pointed to the puddle of his phlegm, and shouted, "Asshole! Asshole!" Maybe it's not that everyone goes mad for a moment or two along the way, but rather that everyone *is* a little bit mad, and occasionally it breaks out like a fiery rash squirming and crawling across your screaming skin before fading away until the next livid outbreak. Madness is evanescent for the famous, the wealthy, or the lucky, but the crazy girl at my gym hasn't been blessed with fame or fortunate circumstances. She's not a squirrely superstar whose antics are splashed across the pages of glossy pop culture publications and colorful entertainment websites to the delight of adoring fans. Her mental distress will never be recorded and written down as a poignant tale of courage in the face of anguish. Madness is her identity, it's who she has become, it has no expiration date; it's not a limited run. Tomorrow won't free her from the madness. Tomorrow won't find her starring in a major motion picture despite a habit of unruly public behavior. She won't discover a fragile peace with her personal demons or channel her torment into song. Tomorrow will find her, once again, staring blankly out at something only she can see and laughing to herself over a private joke that probably wasn't very funny to begin with.

It only takes a moment…and sometime a moment is just enough. It was the fits of madness torturing Tiberius' paranoid soul when he pondered the terrible life he had lived that allowed me to seep into the cracks and crevices of his fractured mind and thus unleash the permanently, profoundly lunatic Caligula onto an unsuspecting world. Temporarily insane or steadfastly crazy, it doesn't matter; it only takes a moment of madness to do some real damage, and it's in those dark moments that I have waited patiently to whisper and instigate. So let me thank all of the crazy people…there are too many of you to mention by name. Because of you, I've succeeded beyond my wildest imagination and tormented this world more than I ever dreamed possible. You've made me the vampire I am today. I couldn't have done it without you.

DODGING ICEBERGS

Time is difficult to measure. Listening to a person talk about her grandchild's adorable antics can seem to drag on endlessly, yet it feels like only yesterday that I first heard the startling news of the Titanic's demise when in fact more than a century has already passed since the legendary ship sank. "Anniversary" is the word used to describe the tragedy's various milestones, but given the flood of trinkets, souvenirs, movies, documentaries, books, magazine articles, and jewelry that accompany any mention of the doomed luxury liner, "jubilee" would probably be a better term. Eyewitness accounts painted a murky and often conflicting picture of the Titanic's grand finale, but if the events had unfolded today, the black ocean would have twinkled with tiny specks of blue light as survivors recorded the details of the ship's final moments on their cell phone cameras from the safety of the lifeboats, and a spellbound world-wide audience could have watched the frigid carnage over and over and over again on YouTube and Instagram.

Captain Smith should have dodged icebergs, but instead he tried to sail into the history books on a trans-Atlantic record.

Had he achieved his intended accomplishment, I doubt that anyone but maritime enthusiasts would have remembered the speed of his journey, much less his ship's name, but the Titanic's ill-fated skipper bumped heads with eternity when his hopes for triumph turned into tragedy. Nine times out of ten, tragedy trumps triumph in the popular imagination. People love a tragedy, and the bigger and grander, the better, but any misfortune, no matter how small, will still bring a certain measure of satisfaction to even the casual observer. It's the climactic failure, the final heartbreak, the suffering that punctuates the preceding promise that makes people feel better about their own disappointing lives. Tragedy without romance or sweeping scope is just your own tawdry story – sad and petty – so wars, riots, revolutions, celebrated murders, plagues, natural disasters, assassinations, and falls from power all get dressed up in high-end finery, adorned and gilded for popular consumption. When pulled back for a wide-screen Panavision view, just about anything can be made to look heroic, but zoomed in uncomfortably close, even the good fight is dirty work, and the real horror of tragedy presents itself. That's when tragedy sneaks up behind you, crowds beside you, and shows you its true face.

Many years ago I made the acquaintance of a grizzled blue-collar WWII veteran named Hank. Although Hank had been awarded the Purple Heart and the Silver Star for the blood he had shed and the bravery he had shown, he never rose up through the ranks and had spent the conflict as a lowly soldier crawling through the mud until he returned home and toiled for the rest of his life as a factory worker who lived in a modest bungalow and drove Oldsmobiles. But those several war years loomed large over his thoughts and forged his personal identity as an everyday hero. "We had to go through and sweep the area. The Germans had already high-tailed it out, but we had to make sure they were all gone," he told me of his service in Europe during the war's waning days. "The little farm houses, the fields, everything had to be checked, so we were poking around in a barn, and I'll be damned if there wasn't a Kraut soldier hiding in there – a young one, no more than sixteen. He didn't think we could see him, but we did, so my buddy Joe lifts his rifle and puts a bullet right through the kid's head," Hank said, tapping a place above his eye with a finger. "We walked over to the body, and Joe, he picks up a goddamn rake and shoves the handle end into the bullet hole, and that damn kid's body starts to jerk and wiggle like he was plugged in!" Hank laughed. "It was the damndest thing I ever saw." "Sixteen?" I asked. He fell silent for a moment, then lightly touched his forehead with a calloused hand and whispered, "My grandson is sixteen." Crowding out the triumph he'd carefully nurtured in his own mind was a quiet little trage-dy stripped of any grandiloquence. Decades after he played his small part in history, Hank's most vivid personal memory of the proceedings was the bullet to the head of a frightened teenager trying to hide from the horror. The world's epic disasters might capture the imagination, shape political beliefs, cause kingdoms to fall or nations to rise. They might define an era and set civili-zation on a new course, but the little tragedies, the personal ones that play out day after day, haunt the soul and kill the spirit piece by piece. I've been around a long time, a very long time – since before the Prophet moved the mountain, before Christ arrived to conquer the world, before the god of Israel rose bitter and resentful from the desert's choking heat – and I can tell you that people have always been a vicious, cruel animal…and every bit as bad now as they were way back then. Styles change, attitudes adjust, and weapons get shinier, but the meanness is in the DNA. You can find the cruelty everywhere – in the darkest night or the loveliest spring day.

Spring has been unusually balmy with a number of days

reaching summer-like temperatures. I was on the bus one warm evening last week, and several stops after I boarded, a heavy-set girl stepped on dressed from head to toe in summer clothes. She wore white elastic-waistband pleated pants, a bright orange and yellow floral top with short cap sleeves, sensible flat sandals, and a wide-brimmed hat. For some reason she looked very happy – not as if a particular event that had just occurred, but more generally, as if she expected life to take a turn for the better with the arrival of nice weather. She was like a big, pastel blossom opening up to a new day as she searched for the fare card in her purse. "Come on, fat ass! Move it!" The voice cut sharply through the air, and the heavy girl froze; her pink face sagged, and her eyes sparkled with watery panic as the passengers all looked up at once and turned their attention towards the front of the bus. "Jesus! Come on, move your fat ass already!" said the voice belonging to a young man in cargo shorts and a faded t-shirt printed with the logo of a university known more for its party atmosphere than curriculum. He reached around the fat girl with his own fare card and repeated, "Jesus!" while the bus driver stared straight ahead as if nothing had happened. "Excuse me!" the young man's companion, a slightly unwashed and hungover-looking blonde in skinny jeans and a baby-T, said loudly, and she followed her boyfriend down the aisle. There was nothing interesting about the couple. They possessed an appearance that was too bland to make them noteworthy, but what they lacked in natural attributes they made up for with an almost frightening sense of confidence, and it was that confident air that deflected attention away from their own boorish behavior and towards the object of their ridicule. People looked at the girl in her colorful summer outfit, and some smirked slightly while a few others shook their heads in a defensive measure to shield their own insecurities and personal shortcomings from unwelcome scrutiny.

The door closed with a malicious hydraulic hiss, the bus lurched forward, and the fat girl lost her balance as she lumbered towards the empty seat next to me.

For some reason, I attract misery like a magnet; I always have, and I initially expected that I'd be required to give the girl a blunt talking-to about life's wickedness, but it would be a safe bet to say that she was already well aware of anything I might tell her. She sat down, adjusted her blouse, and silently looked forward as if she were mentally trying to remove herself, to project herself to a place that was kinder and more pleasant. The occupants of the bus returned to their books and texting and quiet conversations. Then, suddenly, a sound like cows lowing drifted up the aisle. The young couple nudged each other, giggled, and directed another round of "Mooo" towards the fat girl. Tension returned, and the atmosphere again grew heavy with anxiety as people shot sideways glances filled with an odd mix of derision and dread towards the still and silent girl sitting next to me. Their movements were slight, almost imperceptible, but everyone began to turn, to rotate in one direction or another to remove themselves as best they could from the situation, hoping that life's cruelty might not suddenly notice them. People love a tragedy, just not their own, and the malice directed at a person whose only offense was extra weight and an unfortunate personal sense of style cut too close to the bone for the passengers to engage with the cruel spectacle. The fat girl abruptly stood and hurried off the bus only two short stops after her arrival, and as the bus went on its way, I turned and watched her from the window. Shoulders slumped, head lowered, she walked down the street in the direction she had come from, back to wherever she called home, dodging icebergs as best she could.

FRIENDS

When the seasons change, many people rummage through their closets and weed out pieces of their wardrobe that have become dated, worn, or ill-fitting. The world's natural rhythm of rest and rebirth sparks a desire to wipe the slate clean and start over fresh. I go through my closet of friends at regular intervals, but I don't let the first appearance of crocuses or the yellowing of leaves dictate my motivation to toss out the trash. As styles evolve and culture shifts, so does the usefulness of friendships, and there is no point in maintaining an association when it reaches the "Remember when we…" point. My past is prodigious, my future is forever, and I'd rather surge forward than stall out and stagnate, so the last thing I want is a weary load of shelf life-expired friends dragging me down until they age, wither, and die off like tattered old parakeets. I've always had an uneasy friendship with the concept of "friendship." Even during that brief moment in time when I was normal, ordinary—like you; I never desired close personal attachments unless I needed help lifting something of exceptional weight or wanted to share a particularly malicious story about a mutual acquaintance. Over the ages, many friends have floated in and out of my life, serving various purposes, and I choose my friendships no differently than I choose my clothes...and I discard them just as easily. Many people assume that I'm part of some shadowy network of the undead that meets in dark, spooky places and engages in eternal political struggles and *Peyton Place*-like personal dramas, but truth is always less colorful than fiction, and reality much duller than myth. You wouldn't want to watch a movie or read a book about your own life or that of your neighbors or co-workers without considerable embellishment. I'm no different. Stripped of the ornamental filigree and rigid requirements dictated by legend, my existence is far less fanciful than folklore and pop culture would have you believe. There aren't many of my kind; I'm part of a very rare breed, and you'd stand a better chance of spotting a nearly-extinct Lear's macaw in Central Park during the dead of winter than encountering a vampire. Every once in a great while I will feel the sensation of being watched, and I'll spy a pair of dark eyes staring at me through a crowd. After a moment of silent acknowledgement, like a cobra and viper warily avoiding each other, we move on. No society or caste system of vampires exists, no nation or social club of the *nosferatu*...but there is my one true friend, Sebastian.

Sebastian has been my friend for over a thousand years, and though we share little in common, it's the attributes that make us so different that have kept us close, even if decades pass between the times when we share our company. He possesses the type of dark-haired, chiseled good looks that have been desirable ever since man first stood erect and square-shouldered, and my natural inclination upon our initial meeting would have been jealousy or a measure of resentfulness but for the fact that my friend has never used his august physical qualities in an offensively vain manner. Indeed, he's often mystified as to why people are so drawn to him. We were at the famous Peppermint Lounge in New York City one night in 1960 when Sebastian was asked for an autograph by a young man who had been following us around the club. "There you go," Sebastian said with some confusion and more than a little embarrassment as he handed over a signed napkin. But the "fan" tossed the souvenir into an empty highball glass on the bar and said, "I thought you were John Gavin," as he walked away without looking back. I've never been asked for an autograph or mistaken for the likes of Mr. Gavin. My appearance is made up of a collection of sharp angles and pointed features that can be attractive or striking – even compelling under the right conditions – but I could never claim to be handsome, and while I would describe myself as "intense," I have to admit that a consensus of opinions formed over the ages considers me to be "sneaky-looking." Unlike me, Sebastian always needs to be surrounded by a group of buddies, and though friendship comes easily to him, and though he tries with great effort, he never fits in or finds a true place with the people he has met over the centuries.

"Do we have to wear sweatpants?" I asked when Sebastian invited me to a Super Bowl party. "Oh, no…no, it's not that sort of crowd," he said. "I think you'll like them…at least some of them…maybe one or two." Sebastian acted as though the invitation was a kindness, a nice gesture that he wanted to direct my way to ease my solitude. I was updating him on my latest exploits when he shook his head, interrupted, and said, "Alexios, you're like that dark cloud that follows people around on the Abilify commercials." I've been called many things – a demon, a dark angel, a fallen angel, a devil, the Devil, a scourge, a torment, a curse, a horror, a monster – but I've never before been likened to clinical depression. "I think it will do you some good to socialize," he said, but I knew in reality that he wanted me to accompany him so he wouldn't feel alone in the midst of his new of friends. Friendship can be a lonely place. "They've all known each other for a long time, and they do a lot of things together – movie nights, book readings," Sebastian told me as the sun dropped low enough in the sky for us to head out to the party. But my spirits sank along with the sun as I imagined a pretentious discussion centered around a John Grisham novel. "We won't have to watch something on PBS after the game, will we?" I inquired with genuine concern, but Sebastian assured me of that event's unlikeliness.

I don't recall Egyptian nobility asking people to bring a covered dish to their banquets, and I can assure you that Truman Capote didn't request a potluck offering from the glitterati attending his famed Black and White Ball, so I'm somewhat put-off by the current trend of requiring invited guests to arrive for an event with the very things that normally fall under basic hosting obligations, but, regrettably, Sebastian and I found ourselves at the deli counter of an upscale and over-priced supermarket trying to guess what average people like to eat. Sebastian pointed to a glass bowl of barbecue Buffalo wings nestled in some dark, curly kale leaves. "What is that?" he asked. "I can't be certain, but it looks like aborted fetuses," I said to the horror of customers dressed in various types of football fashions waiting to buy luncheon meats, sliced cheeses, and rotisserie chickens. We felt it was best to step away and head to a friendlier section of the store. "People like to get drunk," I said as we made our way the liquor aisle, where I picked up a bottle of wine. Sebastian immediately said, "No! They talk about wine all the time. They're pretty serious about it…I wouldn't want to bring something that might…well…offend them." An intense dislike for Sebastian's new crowd was already welling up inside of me without yet having had the pleasure of personal introductions, so I reached for a bottle of Bombay Sapphire and said, "Everyone drinks gin, even the pope." Sebastian grasped my shoulder, leaned in close, and whispered, "Where did you hear that?!" I just shook my head and waved the question off. We were heading to the checkout line when Sebastian hesitated and said, "I'm not sure about liquor. What if someone is an alcoholic? I don't know these people that well." It took strident convincing on my part, but eventually we left the store with the gin and a "just in case" plastic liter bottle of Fanta.

Sebastian checked the addresses as we made our way down the street, stopped in front of a new-construction townhouse artlessly designed to feign a vintage look amidst immaculately maintained graystones nearly a century old, and said, "Okay, this is where Dennis and Annette live." Annette answered the door and said in a happy tone with an artificial, tinny quality to it, "Hi! Glad you made it…take off your shoes and come in." Sebastian quickly bent over without looking at me and began to untie his shoelaces while I stood for a moment and glared icily at Annette. Once shoeless, we were welcomed in and led through the crowded townhouse. Small TVs were placed in each room, although no one was paying any attention to the game. "Dennis, look who's here…Sebastian and his friend," Annette said to her husband in a manner that sounded as if Sebastian had crassly broken some unspoken rule by bringing me along unannounced. Dennis was standing with a group of guests who all appeared to be in the obnoxious couple's thrall. As Sebastian handed the bottle of gin to Annette, she shrieked, "Bombay! It's so 80s! I love it!" Everyone laughed sharply in agreement until I presented Dennis with the Fanta. An uncomfortable silence gripped the little gathering before Annette asked Sebastian and myself if we would like some wine. "It's really good," she said. "Really good. We just bought it at a tasting last week." "No, thank you," I smiled. I pointed to the bottle of Fanta in Dennis' hand and said, "I'll have some of that." Annette and Dennis exchanged a look—*that* look—and attempted to disappear into the kitchen, but considering the open floor plan they chose for their townhouse, disappearing was impossible, and I could see them obviously trading harsh words about me over the granite-topped island. They returned and handed us the Fanta that would never touch our lips, in glasses of a strangely tilted and lopsided design that were nearly impossible to hold with any comfort. "Nordstrom," Annette said. Dennis resumed the story he was telling before our arrival had interrupted him, and it took me a moment to catch my bearings and understand exactly what he was talking about. "I've never fucked like that before. I mean, she was like a machine…a fucking machine. We dated for six months, and that's all we did…fuck." Annette took a taste of her really good wine through a stretched smile. "That's like my old boss," she said, cutting Dennis off. "I'd walk into his office, close the door, climb on his desk, and say, 'Now!' and we'd do it right there. Every morning before anyone else got in, at lunch time, after work…I've never had such spectacular sex in my life." Dennis described the incredible sex he would have with his second cousin, and Annette answered back with stories about tantric screwing with her best friend's dad. Neither member of the couple looked capable of engaging in sexual activity beyond the lights-out, under-the-cover variety, so their premarital exploits didn't ring true, but that wasn't the point. Their friends enjoyed the tales immensely, even as the smiles on Dennis' and Annette's faces grew tighter and angrier. I was tempted to hand each a knife and tell them to settle this thing once and for all. Sebastian leaned over and suggested that maybe we should "circulate…you know, mingle."

Moving from room to room, Sebastian joined one small clique, then another, but he hovered uncomfortably on the edges and never fully joined in. He smiled or nodded thoughtfully or laughed at all of the appropriate times, but when his arms weren't folded tightly over his chest, his hands were buried deep in his pockets. I avoided the groups and searched out people on their own – the stragglers, the ones staring at the artwork hung on the wall or standing alone, idly taking sips of their drinks. In solitude there is honesty. Not much prodding was required, just a certain amount of finesse, and soon I was learning all about the true nature of these tangled friendships. A woman named Jerri discretely pointed to her friends William and Barry and then unloaded a vicious torrent of unpleasant personal information. Several minutes later I managed to draw some unflattering insights about Jerri from William as Barry nodded enthusiastically in agreement. Petty slights, profound betrayals, and rancors that had aged like a cheap wine unfolded as one by one, each guest at a time, I made my way through the rooms with the Super Bowl grinding on endlessly like a dull hum in the background. I bartered each scrap of acrimony I had gathered for a new story until the bitterness and resentments began to overlap and spread like a poison coursing through the veins and arteries of a helpless body. The groups of guests closed in more tightly together, and a head would turn and stare angrily as someone left the room. The sound of conversation and laughter faded away and was replaced with the hiss of whispers, and soon hostility opened up like a festering sore. An angry voice in the kitchen was drowned out by an even louder, "I don't give a fuck what you think! You're a liar, you always have been a liar!" A woman marched through the living room waving her arms and shrieking, "I don't want to talk about it! I don't want to talk about it!" She wrestled with her coat and shouted to her boyfriend, "Where's my goddamn purse?!" Chaos descended on the townhouse. My work completed, it was time for Sebastian and me to leave.

"Are those Cuban heels?" Sebastian asked as we sat on the front porch and put on our shoes. "Yes," I said, tying my laces. "If I knew I had to take my shoes off, I would have worn different pants. Did you see how long they looked when I was walking around in there?" "I guess I didn't know any of them very well, after all," Sebastian said, making no effort to hide what might have been embarrassment, or maybe disappointment. "They all seemed so nice when I first met them." "They always seem so nice," I said patting Sebastian on the knee. "People always seem like something they aren't...except you. You're like a clean pane of glass that I can see straight through—nothing hidden, nothing blurred." Sebastian stood up, adjusted his coat, and smiled. "Don't be so smug, Alexios, you might be a great mystery to the world, but not to me, mister—and you never have been." We walked down the dark street, anxious to get away from the townhouse, the sniping guests, the Super Bowl, and the non-stop string of loud commercials. "Did you notice how mean Annette was to all of the other women?" Sebastian asked. "Yeah," I said, "and I noticed she colors her own hair, too. I looked in their linen closet and found some Clairol Nice 'n Easy..." Once at the intersection, we said our goodbyes, and I knew years would pass before we might see each other again. Sebastian climbed into a cab and waved to me from the window, and, with a sudden rush of melancholy, I watched the taxi carry my friend away.

BLASPHEMY

IN THE BEGINNING

"In the beginning was the Word, and the Word was with God, and the Word was God."
–John 1:1

In the beginning there was the Word…but was it a good word enunciated with sparkling optimism, or was it a bad word clammy with gloom and doom and reeking with the already-rotting stink of resentment? That's not a trivial question or parlor game to be played out in snobby salons. It's not a transcendental concept to be argued with passion by philosophers and academics. No beginning is ever ambiguous. Things start off either on the right foot or the wrong, and whichever provides that fateful first step dictates the direction the beginning will follow through to the end. So was the word a good one or a bad one? "Awesome!" sets the scene for a story far different than does "Shit!"

People prefer the comforting idealism of the beginning over that of the end, and it's been that way since the dawn of civilization. "A whole new day," "a fresh start," and "the best is yet to come" sound more pleasing than "the final curtain" or "the end of the line," and as the credits roll at the conclusion of a long-await-ed blockbuster movie, audience members watch anxiously for the hint of a preface to the sequel certain to follow. With the ex-ception of devising increasingly dreadful ways to deal out death, mankind's most enduring fascination has always been with the beguiling, unfathomable beginning of it all. Thanks to brilliant scientists, astronomers, geologists, and astrophysicists, we now know all about the Big Bang, black holes, rocky orbs and giant balls of gas whirling through space, shifting continental mass-es, and the 4.5 billion year age of this planet we call home, but before there were telescopes and satellites, intricate instruments and carefully controlled chemical reactions, complicated equa-tions and manipulated neutrons and protons, people had to ex-plain things in more simple, albeit colorful, terms, and so the ancient Creation myths were born during the confused days of antiquity. With little more than the ability to survey their imme-diate surroundings and peer heavenward, the great thinkers and crack-pots of the distant past had little choice but to explicate the natural order of the world in the most extravagantly ridic-ulous of fashions, with mighty deities clashing and battling and causing the mountains to rise up, the seas to fill, and the stars to be flung glittering across the night sky. Thousands of years ago (even without the luxury of readily accessible scientific find-ings, *National Geographic,* and the Discovery Channel) I nev-er believed those cock-and-bull stories, and when I looked at a mountain, I saw nothing more than a natural formation of rock and stone, but most people back then embraced the popular sto-ries with conviction until science and technology began to set the record straight. Downgraded, reclassified, and relegated to ancient history textbooks, the various myths of Creation are now all but forgotten...except for one.

"*In the beginning God created the heaven and the earth. And*

*the earth was without form, and void; and darkness was upon
the face of the deep. And the Spirit of God moved upon the face
of the waters. And God said, Let there be light: and there was
light. And God saw the light, that it was good: and God divided
the light from the darkness. And God called the light Day, and
the darkness he called Night. And the evening and the morning
were the first day."*
–Genesis 1:1.

"Let there be this, let there be that...and that and that and
that..." The Almighty sounded like he was doling out instructions to painters or landscapers, not bringing forth the Universe.
The Jews' take on the weighty enterprise of Creation was by far
the laziest and least imaginative of the lot.

A flick of the wrist, a snap of the divine fingers, and light and
dark were instantly divided into two neat halves. Without effort
or strife, earth and water formed a landscape. Flora blossomed
and bore fruit while fauna of all types sprang forth and engaged
in behavior that shared little in common with the savage day-to-
day grind of eat-or-be-eaten that drives nature in its true form.
Back in the day, I was more highly visible than I am now, and
my public presence was such that I provided the inspiration for
a handful of archaic diabolical demons and malignant spirits.
Some of the characterizations strayed a considerable distance
from the source material while others cleaved closer, but all of
my fictionalized forms were placed in appropriately flashy and
exotic tableaux, so it was no surprise when I learned that even
the dour and self-obsessed Hebrews created a small but vital
role based on me for their grim and oppressive Book of Genesis.
There can be no denying that the serpent is the true star of the
Old Testament's Creation fantasy. Before the adroit snake made
his cameo appearance, Adam and Eve capered naked in Eden

and frolicked and fucked with no shred of embarrassment...and no clue that Yahweh was just a dirty old man in the sky amusing himself by leering at their uninhibited cavorting.

The Word might have ushered in the beginning, but afterward the serpent delivered a no-nonsense, much needed earful to Adam and Eve, and once they covered their money-makers with fig leaves and began to do the nasty in the discrete privacy of the bushes, God became very angry...as angry as you get when you come home after a tough day at work, log onto your favorite porn website, and discover that you're suddenly being asked for a credit card number. The serpent flipped the switch and turned The Garden of Eden's formerly free webcam show into a pay-per-minute subscription service, and there's been hell to pay ever since. All of the ancient musings on the world's origin were silly, to be sure, but there was a primitive awareness in many of those tales of the need for cataclysmic events to shape the environment of existence and then populate it with an array of inhabitants, but that sense of majesty and wonderment is absent from Genesis. It's simply a sordid, anxiety-ridden, psychosexual wallow in blame and guilt and shame that doesn't appeal to man's basic instinct for curiosity, but rather to his basest instinct to head for the gutter. The Book of Genesis has proved to be as enduring as a persistent rash, and over the ages it has managed to dodge the bullet of reason countless times. To this day, even in a nation as advanced and sophisticated as the United States, people cling defiantly to the fable, claiming it as fact. The scummy and seedy saga that kicks off the Old Testament isn't so much an explanation of how the Universe came to be as it is a mirror held up to the sorry spectacle of human nature. That's why so many people feel possessive of its value. It might not be history, but it is your story in many sad ways, from the deceptions and betrayals to the revenge, retribution, and bloodshed.

In the beginning there was the Word, but creeping up behind that lexeme, there is always the promise of another new dawn, and for that there is a calendar. As a new year commences, everyone in the office orders a fresh desk calendar, people buy daily planners to keep in their bags, and they hang wall calendars illustrated with images of cats, cars, cheesecake, beefcake, landscapes, rock stars, or tasteful black and white photography. Clean, unsullied…months of pristine, blank white squares, a day-by-day promise of things to come, but immediately everyone scratches and scrawls all sorts of useless information that fills up as many empty days as possible with reminders of birthdays, vacation days, opening day, appointments, lunch dates, and the anniversaries of milestones both happy and sad. I have no use for calendars. I was born in the summer and died in the spring, I don't need to make a note of those events beneath the picture of a half-dressed fireman or a Thomas Kinkade painting, and I have enough presence of mind to remember that I've made plans to meet you without scribbling the details down with an exclamation point in a leather-bound datebook. People load up their calendars in a desperate attempt to crowd out life, to keep reality from making its own sloppy, indelible mark on those clean white boxes. Someone will die, someone will say, "I don't think we should see each other anymore," your transmission will fail, and you can depend on an assortment of natural and unnatural disasters to bleed across the pages of your calendar. The blood-splattered months of Mogadishu and Aleppo, the bullet-riddled days of Columbine and Newtown began their years as impassive, inscrutable blank spaces waiting patiently to become dates of infamous note. Maybe that's why Genesis continues to resonate. In the beginning people hope for the best, but after countless starts that led to a curdled finish, they've come to expect the worst.

In the beginning there was the Word, but when this whole mess comes to an end, someone will have the last laugh…and at the rate I'm going, it will probably be me. After careful consideration, I've decided that I'll keep things simple as the world takes its bow, and in those final lonely moments of extinction, I'll stare into the gathering void and say, "I told you so."

I'LL BE DAMNED

I own an old, embossed, red leather-bound edition of the New Testament with its page edges extravagantly gilded in gold foil. The text holds no interest for me, but midway through the handsome volume is a series of glossy plates that depict The Stations of the Cross like a gruesome and gory graphic novel rendered in flamboyantly dark and disturbing oil paintings. Hollow-eyed, grimy, and broken, Jesus suffers against a hellish landscape of jagged pitch blacks, dirty grays, and deep browns smudged together in smoky horror laced with blood – a torture-fetish study of bleak agony, splatter, and spray. Contemporaries of the preacher were quite familiar with the ghastly spectacle of crucifixion, and most common folk were haunted by the very real possibility that one day they might end up on the bad end of the cross for even a minor infraction. Nonetheless, many people relished the sight of a sweating, gasping hooligan crucified on a crowded street to die for his sins and his sins alone. A century before The Son of God made his splashy exit on the cross, I watched ordinary people – men, women, young, and old – jeer and throw trash at a beaten, bloody, naked unfortunate who had been suffering for days nailed to jumbled rough planks of wood propped against a wall in one of Beroea's twisting, turning alleyways. "He was your neighbor, wasn't he?" I asked in a voice devoid of any accusatory tone or trace of disapproval. Several people shifted uncomfortably in place, then slunk away into the night, but the rest continued with their fun – unruffled, unperturbed by my observation. Agony is a perennially popular attraction, and I'm convinced the enduring popularity of Christianity rests with the blood and guts climax to the Carpenter from Galilee's tale. Suffering is a spectator sport, and it always has been. Crowds would begin to gather hours before the dreaded Inquisition burned a heretic, and the guillotine's blade in revolutionary France would drop to thunderous applause. When American contractor Nick Berg was beheaded by Islamist militants during the fevered pitch of the Iraq war, people around the world expressed their outrage by watching the video of the hideous event on their computers in the comfort and safety of their homes…multiple times.

Wandering through churches, those temples of gloom and doom, is one of my guilty pleasures—Roman Catholic churches to be specific, but only the old ones…not the modern houses of worship that look like ski lodges or lecture halls. Byzantine and Gothic architectural masterpieces with soaring domes, dark marble, somber, jewel-toned stained glass, and shadowy alcoves dimly lit with flickering red votive candles provide the perfect spaces for martyred saints, sacrificed saviors, and Satan-battling angels to brood. I felt disappointment wash over me the moment I walked into the grand old church and saw a sleek cross fashioned from two tubes of brushed nickel set into a simple square teak base behind the altar instead of a huge crucifix with an anguished Christ twisting in lifelike torment. Many old churches have retro-fitted their lavishly oppressive interiors with au courant trappings, and as I looked around from the vestibule to the altar, I noticed the sleek brushed nickel and teak motif everywhere…even the Stations of the Cross lining the walls had been unfortunately updated in the cold, crisp materials. I joined a small group of elderly parishioners who were waiting for their priest to arrive and begin the services that are a Friday night tradition during Lent. Father DeSando, a man in his late thirties or early forties who looked surprisingly fit and a bit randy, swept down the aisle and greeted us with a silent, boyish smile. "Good evening," he whispered, then he eyed me suspiciously, but not, I might say, disapprovingly. "Does everyone have a booklet?" he asked, holding up a handful of small, staple-bound paper pamphlets with a crown of thorns surrounding the words "The Stations of the Cross" on the cover. The assembled seniors nodded in unison, and, ignoring my raised hand, Father DeSando fished a small metal clicker out of his pocket. *Click.* The group turned, faced the First Station, knelt, blessed themselves, and rose, some more easily than others, with the second *click*. "The First Station of the Cross: Jesus is Condemned to Death," the priest solemnly intoned. He began to read from his booklet. "My Jesus, the world still has you on trial. It keeps asking who you are and why you make the demands you make…" An old woman in a *Jersey Boys* sweatshirt, perm-a-crease polyester slacks, and white sneakers leaned in towards me and whispered, "What an evil man…Pilate, such a coward." "Oh, no, I wouldn't call him evil. He just wasn't very bright," I said quietly. "I only met the man once, but that was my impression of him. He talked non-stop, all sorts of convoluted philosophical nonsense. I finally asked him, 'What is truth?' but he just stared at me. Obviously, though, the question stuck in his mind." The old woman regarded me as blankly as had Pilate. "He was incredibly handsome," I said. "I think that's how he got his post in Judea." The gray-haired lady frowned in confusion and turned to the teak plaque on the wall labeled

"FIRST" in a san-serif font. "That really doesn't do him justice," I said, pointing as discreetly as possible to the infamous procurator represented as a brushed nickel stick figure.

"We adore you, oh Christ, and we bless you because by your holy cross you have redeemed the world," Father DeSando prayed as we approached the Third Station. Bowing his head, he announced, "Jesus Falls the First Time," but before the priest could continue, I whispered and nodded towards the Third Station's plaque, "I've seen some people take really nasty falls – worse than that." The woman in the *Jersey Boys* sweatshirt grabbed my sleeve and said with great excitement, "OH! I took a bad fall in my kitchen the other day! I couldn't get up. Luckily, my daughter was on her way over to take me to Wal-Mart. I could have been laying there for..." "I slipped on a grape at Cosco," a lady wearing a top decorated with small plastic jewels courtesy of the Bedazzler she received as a Christmas gift interrupted. "I thought I broke my hip!" she continued. "Thank God I didn't, but I had a bruise from my behind to my knee. My son-in-law took pictures of it and sent them to a lawyer he knows." The Fourth Station of the Cross: Jesus Meets his Mother. "Here comes trouble," I murmured. "That's right," a woman named Lydia said sourly. "Mine just turned 97. I know it's a blessing to still have her, but it's always something – this hurts or that hurts, I need this, I need that...I don't have minute for myself," she grumbled. Father DeSando rubbed his temple and made his way as quickly as possible through the Fifth and Sixth Stations, but as Veronica Wiped the Face of Jesus, a woman holding a large Sea World tote bag passed a small plastic bottle of anti-bacterial hand cleanser around the group and cautioned, "Those grade school kids were just in here. Who knows if they wash their hands after they do their business?" I smiled, patted her arm and said, "Thank you."

"Even with help, Jesus stumbles and falls to the ground." Father DeSando reached The Seventh Station of the Cross: Jesus Falls the Second Time. A portly old gentleman near the back of the group said, "We were on one of those Disney cruises last summer. That damn boat moved so much I couldn't walk straight. I went down hard right on the deck." Everyone shook their heads in sympathy. "I told my wife, 'No more. Next year we go back to Epcot like always'…" he said as Father DeSando cut him short with the clicker, and we quickly continued on our way through the Savior's Passion. I was about to alert the priest that he had omitted the Ninth Station, Jesus Falls the Third Time, but I understood why he might have deliberately passed that one by, so I kept my peace. "We adore you, oh Christ, and we bless you because by your holy cross you have redeemed the world," Father said in a faltering voice. He cleared his throat and forged ahead to The Tenth Station: Jesus is Stripped of his Garments. Haltingly, he read from the little pamphlet held in his trembling hand, "Part of the indignity is to be crucified naked." I turned, faced the group, and spoke not a word but simply raised a provocative eyebrow. "Ugggh!" a woman named Pat groaned. "I'm sick of this naked business everywhere nowadays! We rented a movie with that Justin Timberlake the other night, and there he was in the altogether. We turned it off." "I started my computer this morning," an old man in a Members Only jacket announced, "and I saw a commercial for Amborcommie & Fish with these fellas wrestling and kissing in the shower." A collective gasp rose, and the man added, "I hollered to my wife, 'Did someone put porn on this damn machine?!'" His wife nodded her head in agreement and said, "It was terrible…just disgraceful." "Some of the costumes on Dancing With the Stars," Pat began to say, but another woman cut her off and informed the group that she no longer watches Hollywood award shows because, "All you see are these gals falling out of their dresses like strippers."

I could feel Father DeSando's burning eyes trained on me. No doubt his priestly powers enabled him to identify me as the ancient evil presence, the devil, the timeless enemy, the wicked trickster who had arrived uninvited and violated the holiness of his church...although a simple process of elimination probably factored in quite heavily as well. He glared at me with open contempt, clicked angrily several times to silence his parishioners, then marched away, spun quickly in a swirl of black cassock, faced the altar, genuflected, and disappeared into the sacristy. "Father, Father, why have you forsaken me?" ...and we were forsaken, abandoned by Father DeSando. Rudderless, leaderless, I feared chaos could descend on the little group and that a geriatric *Lord of the Flies*-like nightmare played out amongst the pews might erupt at any moment, so I seized control of the situation, waved my hand in a soothing yet authoritative manner and said, "Ladies and gentlemen, The Eleventh Station: Jesus is Nailed to the Cross.

"Crucifixion as a form of execution was invented by the Persians but used in a far simpler—you might even say 'demure'—format than the Romans would later employ. I gave the Persians my advice freely; I told them to dress it up, make it an event, but they weren't very open-minded to suggestions," I informed the parishioners. "The Romans, on the other hand? They listened to me and turned crucifixion into a mighty big show," I continued, having abandoned completely the little Stations of the Cross booklet. The group gathered around with a renewed interest. "The bastards crowned Our Lord with thorns to mock him," a bald man in a Banlon shirt said, boldly encroaching on my oration. "Actually," I curtly corrected him, "crowning with thorns was a common practice in crucifixions. Crucified prisoners died of asphyxiation. The only way to breathe and therefore stay alive on the cross was to pull yourself up, so I told the Romans, 'Don't make it easy, this isn't a party,' and they began to wind thorns around the victims' heads, making it unspeakably painful to push against the rough wood. Brutal, to be sure, but an inspired touch, if I might pat myself on the back," I concluded my Eleventh Station lecture. Several people exclaimed, "Oh, my!" or "Really?!" Others whispered excitedly, and the lady in the *Jersey Boys* sweatshirt fished a mint out her purse and said, "I'll be damned!"

NAZARETH, WE HAVE LIFTOFF

The other evening, I saw a teenage girl who was sitting alone in the window seat of a fast-food restaurant known for the considerable heft of its hamburgers reading from a small book of prayers. At certain points throughout the text, she would take a pause from silently mouthing the verses to bow her head and kiss a small gold cross she wore on a thin chain around her neck. She didn't kiss the pendant in the tight-lipped manner people kiss family members on holidays, nor did she adopt the open mouth, spitty version of the kiss associated with lustful sexual congress. The young girl raised the cross to her lips and kissed it much the same way an underage fan might furtively kiss the cheek of a pop star scribbling out an autograph. I detected a trepidation in her act, the dull awareness that she was attempting without success to fully invest herself in a fantasy. No physical abnormality, defect, or infirmity was apparent that might have led a person so young to such a fervent display of devotion, so I was left to wonder if inscrutable and whimsical fate had, for no good reason, decided to rain unhappiness down upon the girl. Maybe she was chosen by her peers to be the outcast, or maybe her family ground every last bit of youthful eagerness out of her. For whatever reason, she sought joyless retreat in the stern demands of the Almighty. Enfilading syllables caused her lips to rapidly twitch and tremble with each vowel and consonant, but no inspirational words took fully formed shape, no true meaning lifted off the pages of her missal. The girl's eyes darted and raced over the collection of letters lined up in neatly ordered rows in her book, and for a moment she was removed from whatever tormented her young life as she rocked back and forth in a robotic glory of God.

When the ancient belief systems faltered and fell in favor of the more streamlined concept of a one true God who sets up and enforces all the rules along a cripplingly narrow parameter, religion lost its sense of fun. The colorful castes of horny deities and flamboyant demons were replaced by a dour and judgmental divine despot and his equally flinty sidekicks. In a multiple choice world, people have been left with a grim theological menu featuring only three main courses: the haughty and self-important Judaism, the bitter and oppressive Islam, and, finally, Christianity. Christianity alone possesses the understanding that religion at its core is a costume drama, not a creed, and its saints and angels, holidays, and fables have cribbed quite shamelessly from the fantastically imagined religions it replaced.

Easter Sunday, the commemoration of Jesus' Resurrection, is the highest Holy Day of the Christian faith, but in practical terms, Christmas eclipses it in every way. Marshmallow Peeps and hard-boiled eggs dyed a variety of pastel hues in baskets filled with shredded cellophane can't compete with iPhones and jewelry hidden beneath festive wrappings and accompanied by gift receipts. Maybe The Passion, with its backstabbing, betrayal, and bloodletting doesn't lend itself to sparkly decorations, holiday cheer, and carols, although Andrew Lloyd Webber cranked out some bouncy pop tunes based on the unpleasant story. Celebrity news and gossip have been guilty pleasures of mine since long, long before there was TMZ, *Entertainment Tonight*, Rona Barrett, *Photoplay*, or Suetonius, but word of the Nazarene's remarkable return from death and subsequent high-flying departure from planet Earth didn't reach me until well after the supposed events occurred, and by that time the story had become so convoluted, entangled, and enmeshed in old tall tales and standard deity myths that I have to believe the real Jesus was rather like Buffalo Bill Cody: an unassuming figure elevated, embellished and recreated as a star attraction by wily dime-store novelists. Forty days after the miraculous resurrection, Jesus ascended into Heaven, and like many gods, he left behind the promise—or threat—of a return that reads far differently than the "Kumbaya" routine he peddled in life. Like something you might see in a dark and sinister fantasy painting or airbrushed on the side of a van, Christians look forward to the Savior's return as a day of fire, brimstone, and savage retribution. Payback time. Turn the other cheek, indeed. Blessed are the vengeful, for their blood lust shall be satiated. Jesus wasn't the first god to ascend to Paradise; in fact, he's not the only major player in Christianity to be outrageously credited with that feat. His mother, the Blessed Virgin Mary, shot to the heavens from a launch pad located in modern day Turkey that has become quite a tourist trap, but I have a feeling Suada is more popular with the well-heeled class of visitors. When mankind first conjured up gods and devils, spirits and sprites to explain the natural workings of the world, the concept was simple and very basic, but as civilizations grew and societies became more complex, so did their gods, and those divine creatures took on more and more human characteristics until the denizens of Olympus began to descend regularly to earth, where they would fraternize and fornicate and otherwise meddle in the affairs of the mortal world. When they finished slumming with the regular folk, Zeus and his crew would ascend back to where they came from. Ascension became a rather mundane occurrence to the Greeks, and likewise, Jesus' leave-taking was scripted as a tastefully understated affair. There was no countdown, no "Nazareth, we have liftoff," no roiling blast of ignited rocket fuel, and no razor sharp white trace of the Savior streaking heavenward. Maybe his return will be flashier.

Resurrection is certainly not a concept foreign to my own personal experience. I rose from the dead, and it didn't take me three days to accomplish the task. My eyes opened, and I was back in business and ready to go in a matter of minutes. The event wasn't accompanied by a radiant flash of light, rolling boulders, or a souvenir shroud left behind with my likeness silk screened on the front and the commemorative date on the back. Fact vs. fiction. Monster vs. Messiah. My rise from the dead is viewed as repulsive, a horror, but the meticulously crafted and message-managed fiction of the Easter story has become a source of salvation for billions of people. Blessed are the needy, for they shall believe anything. The authors of the Bible never asked for my input, but some people have insisted that Jesus' famous quote, "Give not that which is holy unto the dogs, neither cast ye your pearls before swine…" bears my fingerprint, and I must humbly admit they are correct. Two centuries before Jesus preached his gospel, I spoke those very words to an acquaintance in Antioch – Lucius, who had a weakness for Roman soldiers. My context was somewhat different than what ended up in the Holy Scriptures, as I was attempting to cleverly steer Lucius away from my own brawny object of interest, while the same words, when co-opted and placed on the Savior's divine lips, were much less self-serving and lurid. In many ways, however, Jesus and I share some fundamental traits. Neither of us exhibits a shyness when it comes to pontificating our worldviews and philosophies, but Jesus was a huckster hawking his own divine celebrity, while I am simply outspoken.

The living-breathing-of-this-world, flesh-and-blood Jesus was most likely no more than one of those wandering nuts who were a dime a dozen back in that day and time. Preachers, sages, messiahs, magicians, prophets—whatever the hell they were called—some of them dunked people in water, and others warned of the world's imminent destruction. No doubt, the carpenter from Galilee spread his saccharine message of peace and love with conviction, but the carefully crafted, focus-grouped, and manufactured Son of God, Savior, Jesus Christ Superstar was created to sell salvation just like the acne creams, discount car insurance, and erection pills you see advertised on late night TV. For the incredibly low price of your hard-earned cash, your vote, and your soul, you will receive…what—a promise and a prayer? But are you so sure the promise of a heavenly reward, with its royalty and caste system of cherubim and seraphim, saints and martyrs, beatified and blessed, will be any better than this lousy, unfair world? The intent of any religion is meant to ensure the unwashed faithful's acceptance of passive compliance. "Blessed are the meek: for they shall inherit the earth." In all honesty, that's telling you the corner office is yours without having to scratch and claw your way to it inch by brutal inch. The next time your boss informs you that you've been passed over for a promotion, don't expect him to say, "You just weren't meek enough for the position." "Blessed are the pure in heart: for they shall see God." Pureness of heart won't get your foot in the door, much less past the secretary, and don't think for a split second that pureness of heart will get you anywhere near an NFL quarterback or famous guitarist. "Blessed are you when others revile you and persecute you and utter all kinds of evil against you falsely on my account."

It's not difficult to imagine a sleazy, greasy political hack running for office reciting those words at a humid campaign appearance somewhere in the Deep South. Blessed are the gullible, for they can be taken advantage of.

For the sake of argument, let's say that Jesus did rise from the dead in splashy Broadway splendor and then shot into the heavens like a bottle rocket. If you believe someday you'll be hobnobbing inside the Pearly Gates with Mr. Christ, I've got some bad news for you. You can't pal around with Jack Nicholson, you can't even "friend" one of the lesser Kardashians on Facebook, so what makes you think that you can party in Paradise with its biggest star? That's the most exclusive club of all. Security will stop you long before you even make it to the line of servile angels and saints forming behind velvet ropes. No matter how damn virtuous, no matter how meek or kind, you will never get to hang out with Jesus and Elvis in the VIP lounge, so have another drink, buy yourself something nice, get laid. It's the best you can hope for...believe it.

BLESS ME ALEXIOS,
FOR I HAVE SINNED

At my suggestion, Napoleon grabbed the bejeweled crown from the hands of a stunned Pope Pius VII and coronated himself Emperor of the French at the extravagant ceremony held in his honor at Notre Dame Cathedral. A decade later, following his final defeat at Waterloo, I forbade him to grovel before his victors. "I appeal to history!" Napoleon defiantly announced as he disappeared into exile on St. Helena. Forgive me not, indeed.

Forgiveness: the concept confounds me, its purpose perplexes me. Depending on which side you find yourself, forgiveness is either the cherry on top or a bitter pill to swallow. Bestowing forgiveness lavishes a serene righteousness on a person too weak-willed to seek proper retribution. Begging forgiveness is nothing more than a last-ditch effort to salvage a situation after a carefully crafted scheme has gone horribly awry. Forgiveness is an armistice signed under the most demeaning conditions, and it sets up a perpetually unbalanced dynamic. The chastened forgiven is never allowed to forget the self-serving benevolence of his enemy. To be sure, forgiveness is a spineless, passive-aggressive victory at best. I have neither granted nor beseeched forgiveness, and I have never turned the other cheek...unless I needed a few minutes to catch my breath, collect my thoughts, and plan my revenge. Forgiveness is no private affair, it isn't a back room deal or a top secret negotiation; forgiveness can only take flight as a public spectacle carried out for all to see...a pageant of humiliation and hollow triumph. When you prostrate yourself for pardon you sign away the house, cash in your last chip, bare your neck, and throw in the towel.

With sagging faces, bowed heads, and clasped hands they came to seek forgiveness. Parishioners scattered amongst the pews in the grand old church knelt in silent prayer as the Lenten season drew to a close and Holy Week approached, and I doubt many of them prayed for the poor, their loved ones, or the well-being and wisdom of the pope and his magnificent Holy See. Instead, under the watchful eyes of their Savior and the martyred saints rendered in glittering, deep-hued stained glass, they most likely came that night to brood over their own shameful and disappointing lives. Like a shadow, I drifted around the Gothic church searching its alcoves dimly lit by candles and Medieval-style hanging light fixtures until I came to a stop before the vaguely sinister-looking confessional doors. Bread and wine transformed into the body and the blood of Christ, the washing away of sin...the Catholic Church is steeped in ceremony and divine alchemy, and in the darkness of the confessional, some of the Church's most beguiling magic unfolds. I sat in the dark booth on the little wooden seat where the priest offered forgiveness to his sinful flock – the ritual cleansing of a soiled soul – but the only hocus-pocus in that cramped, pitch-black, closet-like room was the murky magic of the mind. The squeak of hinge and the soft click of a door that had been carefully opened then closed stopped me as I was about to make my way back out into the church. I waited a moment, listened in the darkness, then slid back the small wooden panel on the wall. From the dim light filtering through an ivory colored fabric screen, I could see the blurred shape of a sinner seeking absolution.

A voice, rattling and distressed from too many cigarettes and too many hard years, broke the silence, "Bless me, Father, for I have sinned. It's been…oh, I guess Christmastime since my last confession. "I've had impure thoughts," the old man informed me in a haltering stutter, embarrassed by the sound of his own admission. Taken aback by the gravity of his guilty conscience, I found myself momentarily speechless, and after a pause I said— with little concern for the solemnity of the setting— "Well, who hasn't?" "It's a sin, Father," the elderly man almost whispered, but I settled back down on the small wooden chair and said, "You do realize the most popular Internet search is for porn, don't you?" The troubled parishioner cleared his throat, then said, "Like those dirty pictures and such?" "Exactly!" I said, leaning closer to the translucent screen separating us. "How sinful can it be when so many people are…listen, it's almost as natural as breathing, and that's not a sin, is it?" "I guess not, Father, but…" the old man said sounding a bit defensive, and before he had the opportunity to engage me in a theological argument, I quickly asked, "Who was the object of your impure thoughts?" "I don't want you to think I'm cuckoo or anything…" the old man began. "My wife likes that *Bachelor* show on TV. Every week I complain about it, but I sit right there next to her on the couch and we see it together…" "Oh, yes! I've watched it…but they never pick a very attractive bachelor, except for that guy who owned the bar in Texas," I mused, and the tortured soul in the confessional quickly interrupted me. "I don't know anything about that. I'm talking about…the other ones." "Of course you are, the bachelorettes," I said, nodding my head. "Yes," the old man agreed, getting me back onto the proper track. "They all live together in the big house." "The villa," I corrected, then I allowed him to proceed. "And they're always wearing bathing suits, little ones, you know—bikinis or their underclothes or dresses with almost nothing on top," he explained. "How good do you think the ratings would be if they wore muumuus and sweat suits?" I asked, surprised that I found it necessary to articulate the question. Silence hung in the darkness, then the old man softly groaned and said, "It doesn't seem fair…you know, one man and all of those beauties." "Ahhh, now were getting somewhere," I smiled behind the glowing fabric. "Every week you sit next to your frumpy old wife and…" "She was never much to look at, even back in the day," the old man said with an abruptness that startled me. "Her sister was mighty fine, though," he added with the wistfulness attached to a cherished memory. "You should have tried your luck with her sister when you were young," I said, growing more casual and conversational in tone. "I did!" the old man said. "But she turned me down, and somehow I ended up with the other one." "You settled," I told him flatly. "That's one way of putting it," he said sadly. Then he tried to stop, make a hard turn, and change directions: "Don't get me wrong, here; my marriage is a good one, I'm happy…all things considered." "You settled," I repeated my painfully astute point. "You got me there," the old man sighed with a weary chuckle. "But I guess I knew that all along." He made his way out of the confessional holding the door open for the next troubled soul.

"Bless me, Father, for I have sinned…greed, the sin of greed, Father," the woman's weary voice drifted like a melancholy ghost through the gauzy curtain. I adjusted myself on the hard little chair and leaned against the wall, hoping to find that most elusive position of comfort in the stifling little box of the confessional as the next sinner told me her tale of woe. "I lost three before my daughter Kate was born, and to be honest, every time it happened I felt relieved, you know…relieved. Maybe I wasn't ready. I always had so many plans, so much I wanted to do, but then when Katie came along I was, well, I knew she was a gift from God. She became my whole life," the woman began as a prelude to the admission of her wicked behavior. "Katie's been married for, oh, gosh, almost fifteen years now…seems like forever," she said. "My son-in-law, he was a psychology major – whatever the hell that is – hasn't worked a day since I've known him." "He's a deadbeat," I said, trying to quicken the pace of her confession. "You got that right!" the woman said, her voice taking on a new vibrancy. I sighed and stated the obvious: "Let me venture a guess: you tried to warn her before she said 'I do.'" "You bet I did!" she almost shouted. "But did anybody listen to me?" I heard an agitated rustling from the other side of the screen, then she went on. "They had to have a house, they just fell in love with this house that they had to have…you know who had to cough up the down payment? Me—that's who, and now they can't afford the mortgage." "Times are tough," I said, but through the murky fabric I could see her head shake angrily. "Bull! I've made it through plenty of tough times…" She drew in several deep breaths, and a calm stillness settled in for a moment before her story resumed. "My husband passed away last summer, the end of June," she said quietly. "I felt lost without him, you know, abandoned, but my girlfriends, Cynthia and Pat, said I should move on with my life, get out more, so we're all going on a cruise together." Having lost interest in the woman's stream-of-consciousness personal purge, I decided to melt away into the darkness and escape the claustrophobic confines of the confessional, but the confessor suddenly laid her head against the fabric screen and began to sob, and so my attention sharpened to a keener edge. "Katie says they'll lose the house if I don't give them a hand; she says I should cancel my cruise so I can help them out, but I don't want to help them out…I mean, cancel my trip." Her words flowed as freely as her tears, and any opportunity for me to offer a stinging appraisal of her wretched daughter and worthless son-in-law was lost in the torrent of grief. "I told Katie it was too late for me to get a refund, but she looked up the cruise line on her computer and found out that I can still get my money back," she rasped in a hoarse whisper. "Excuse me, ma'am," I interrupted politely, "I thought you were confessing the sin of greed, but clearly you're also a liar." "What? But…but," she stammered once the shock of recognition had attached itself to my words. "But nothing," I scolded. "If you lied to Katie, why should I believe anything you say?" The woman made a strange noise that I can only describe as the unpleasant union of humiliation, horror, and offense. "I'm sorry; I can't offer you forgiveness at this time," I said in a manner that was more businesslike than benevolent. The woman groaned indignantly, and without absolution, still tainted with the stain of sin, she slammed the confessional door on her way out.

Bless me, Father…for I am unhappy…I am frightened… lonely…for I have wasted my life…for I am nearing the end, and I wish I could start over from the beginning and do everything differently. I spent an hour in that goddamn confessional listening to their pain and disappointment, their failures and fears, and for the first time in my 7000-year existence I felt the ponderous weight of eternity crushing me in the terrible tiny black room. An hour became an unbearable forever, and after a teenage boy sullenly confessed to harboring amorous feelings for his step-sister, I had without question reached my limit of the maudlin misery, the self-indulgent grief and conceited hand-wringing over a-whole-lot-of-nothin' pouring unabated from the parade of penitents. Where were the true villains – the murders and rapists, the thieves, grifters, terrorists, and miscreants? I wondered as I evaporated from the sanctum of contrition and made my way back out into the church. No one had knelt and bowed their head in the dark to beseech the man behind the curtain for exculpation; they wanted someone to listen, to hear the shabby little stories about their dull little lives. "Bless me, Father, bless me, anyone…I'm here, I matter, I'm important even though I've been naughty." Once liberated from the oppressive responsibility of forgiving transgressions, I felt blessedly free – free to go forth and sin myself with zeal and joy. As I made my leave, I heard a muffled voice come from the darkness behind one of the closed confessional doors… "Bless me, Father, for I have sinned…hello? Hello? Is anyone there…?"

WISDOM, PART I

ASK ALEXIOS:
HOW BAD CAN IT HURT?

The ancient Greeks understood that the world is round, and they called our planetary home "the orb." Admittedly, those great thinkers mistakenly believed the sun, the moon, and the stars revolved around the Earth, but half-right is always better than all-wrong. At least they didn't look out onto the horizon and see nothing but an endless flat surface like most cultures did. Way back then and through the ensuing centuries, the world was a mighty big place whose size defied comprehension until man took to the high seas, then to the skies beyond. Soon the world began to shrink, and now with modern technology at our finger-tips, Earth has become almost cramped. These days everyone is accessible – even movie stars, even me.

Maybe it was an irksome twinge of envy, or perhaps I felt left out of the fun, but not long ago I realized the time had come for me to stake out a place on the World Wide Web where I could share my wisdom, spread my gospel, give my what-if and what-for. One of the most curious results of my endeavor was the unexpected appearance of the worried and woebegone, the heartbroken, confused, and misguided seeking my help. Soon my in-box began to fill with their sad little stories and pathetic problems, and I was left with no choice but to offer a few words of council to these troubled souls. I'd like to share a few examples in hopes that you might find comfort in my advice, or at least a measure of amusement in the anguish of others.

LEFT BEHIND

Alexios,

Our neighbors down the street invited me and my husband to a Halloween costume party last Saturday night. My husband, Brad, didn't act very interested in going, so I picked up a costume for him when I went to the Halloween store where Borders used to be. I chose a very cute ladybug costume for myself, and I got Brad a cowboy hat that he could wear with blue jeans and a plaid shirt. Saturday night, I was dressed and waiting for Brad to get ready. I expected to see him in the cowboy outfit I put together for him, but he came down the stairs dressed like Tarzan. His costume was really just flip flops and a silk leopard print scarf I bought at Macy's to wear to my cousin's wedding last spring. I was horrified because it was tied around his waist and barely covered anything. I never lost the weight after I had the twins, and I've gained a few more pounds since then, but Brad still looks like he did when he was twenty. He works out all the time, almost too much, I think. He always looked better than me, and I sometimes feel intimidated by the difference in the shapes we're in. I was really upset when we got to the party and almost started to cry when I saw my girlfriends.

They took me into the kitchen, and I stayed in there with them all evening. The basement was set up like a dance floor with flashing lights, a smoke machine, and loud music. Brad went down there, and I didn't see him again until it was time to leave. He drove the babysitter home, and I went right to bed while he was gone. I'm still not speaking to him, and my friends are all still talking about it. Am I overreacting?

Jill

Jill,

People "dress for success," "dress up," "dress down," and express their individuality through clothes that are mass-produced in sizes to fit any physique, or purchased in dusty resale shops in a contrived attempt to appear bohemian. No one leaves the house without wrapping themselves in some type of self-defining armor; "this is who I am," "this is who I want to be," "this is the best I can do; please be kind." Personal style is more drudgery than fun. Your boss' khaki pants and rolled-up sleeves at the office picnic let you know he's cool, but he's not your friend. His Dockers and polo shirt on casual Friday say, "I understand you little people," but his everyday dark blue suit and striped tie remind you that he's in charge, and don't you ever forget it. The 300-pound high school girl who wears a skintight Tinkerbell t-shirt with "Tink" spelled out in rhinestones across the front is trying to navigate her way through an unforgiving size three world. Clothes are advertisements or denials, deflections or invitations. One way or another, it's all show business, whether smoke and mirrors or a spotlight. Everyone is ready for their close-up, Mr. DeMille. Jill, your real costume is the sweat suit you wear to the shopping mall because you don't want to beg a comparison to the girls in their skinny pants and crop tops. Brad's true costume is the t-shirt that shows off his gym routine and the jeans that fit him like a sin.

Let me guess: you spent the Halloween party camped out in the kitchen hovering near the comfort of the hors d'oeuvre trays filled with cheesy, fatty amuse-bouches along with your friends – a group of shapeless, baggy, bulbous, bitter ladybugs, pumpkins, bumblebees, and Raggedy Annes. Your husband, meanwhile, headed down to the liquor where he bumped and grinded in the smoky, strobe-lit, techno music-throbbing basement with an assortment of fairies, French maids, and pussycats. I don't even want to mention the very real possibility that Brad may have been doing some fancy discotheque dancing with a gym buddy dressed as Apollo in a gold lamé thong and laurel wreath crown. Your Halloween costume said, "I'm sweet and nice, as dull as a Tuesday night and as fragile as a ripe raspberry." Your husband's costume said, "I'm hot and horny, and there's something big waiting for you under this Michael Kors scarf slung around my hips." You both chose your costumes carefully, you both presented the picture you needed to, but Jill, no one really wants nice and sweet. "Nice and sweet" is Miss Congeniality, not Miss Universe; it's a humiliating bone thrown for the loser to chew on, but sometimes that's the best you're given. Upon returning home, you didn't retire to your bed in icy, wordless protest. You simply couldn't bear sitting in the still house, alone and awake, thinking about Brad pulling the car onto a dark side street and climbing into the back seat for a "me Tarzan, you Jane" moment with the babysitter whose own personal choice of "costume" that night was probably intended to arouse your husband's interest. Jill, the silent treatment isn't a punishment. I doubt that Brad paid any attention to your withering disapproval, and in all honesty, he most likely hasn't noticed you much at all in a very long time. The real problem isn't your husband's indecent Halloween get-up. When you saw Tarzan come down the stairs and walk out the door stripped to his basic essence, you realized that Brad had separated the wheat from the chaff – that you had been left behind. Left behind...

Of all my frightful endeavors, I must say the First World War stands as one of my greatest achievements. With all due respect to the archduke, there was no singular event that lit the fuse, there was no one overpowering personality that caused the calamity. No; it was an epic ballet choreographed with nations rising, empires crumbling, political systems changing, and a society unprepared for the savage reality of modern machines of war. It took me years to apply the right movements to all of the principle dancers then put them into place with each role defined, and oftentimes I expected the convoluted scheme to fizzle out before it started. But once I managed to set all the parts and pieces in motion, I sat back and watched from the sidelines as the grand entertainment unfolded. Midway through the conflict I decided an up-close view of the action was in order, so one cold, wet night I arrived like a mist on the Western Front and wandered through the desolation and death of No Man's Land. Combat had ceased for the night, and the eerie silence that settled over the pulverized landscape was broken by the occasional short, crackling burst of machine gun fire somewhere far down the line, followed by a brief eruption of shouting. Then once again, quiet. The soldiers waited in frozen silence in their foul and filthy trenches for the horrors to continue with the dawn of a dreaded new day, and most had left behind any notion of nation and duty and were simply trying to stay alive from one hellish hour to the next.

No Man's Land surrounded me like an expressionist painting realized in oppressive smudges of dirty grays and pitch black – a jumbled and jagged composition rendered in lethal strokes. Once I noticed the first corpse blended into the churned-up earth, I began to see others wherever I directed my attention. Some remained recognizable as men with identities left disturbingly intact, but many more were broken and torn into abstract shapes. "Français? Français?" Suddenly, words like a ghostly whisper floated in the darkness. I turned toward the source of the sound and answered, "*Oui.* Français." The man sighed, a groaning sound of relief, then called out, "I can't reach you. My legs, I can't move my legs...I can't feel anything." Shortly before noon the previous day, a German mortar had exploded several feet from the young Frenchman, blasting away much of the lower portion of his body. He waved his one good hand to me and said, "Pull me up. Once I get back on my feet, I should be fine. I was worried that I had been forgotten...left behind...it's been days...longer...shit, I've been laying here for weeks goddammit... and here you are...we can go back now...we can get the fuck out of here." Time had become a blurred concept to his dying mind, and his thoughts convulsed and spun in a numbed confusion of fragments. The drizzle turned into a drenching cold rain, and the mortally wounded French soldier began to sink in the viscous muck. I reached out and held his hand. "When we get back to the trench, I'll write to my folks," he said, "They're always glad to hear from me, you know, to hear that I'm okay." Only his head, one shoulder, and arm remained visible above his muddy, unmarked grave. "Don't leave me," he said, then he died. I dropped his hand, and he disappeared under the mud and blood and fetid slime. Left behind…

My Great War raged for another two years, and I observed the remainder from a tidier vantage point where I could view the events in terms of strategy, opportunities lost, reversals of fortune and determined perseverance. I never soiled myself with a return to No Man's Land. I left all that behind.

Anthropologists, psychiatrists, theologians, and egotists

would like you to believe that man is the only animal with an awareness of his own mortality, but a deer running from a pack of hungry wolves or a zebra thrashing in the jaws of a Nile crocodile knows death is at its door. Man is the only beast who can't fathom his true place in the larger scheme of things and has fabricated a high and mighty narrative centered on a heavenly reward where he can continue on and on after his mortal remains, left behind, have rotted away. The young French soldier I saw on my visit to No Man's Land wasn't afraid of death. After months on the Western Front he had come to expect a brutal end, but he worried that he would disappear, be forgotten...left behind in a terrible place.

It's not salvation but damnation that captures the imagination and preys heavily on the minds of the worried masses. The damned will be left behind to smolder like crumbling mounds of charcoal, we're told, but in reality everyone is damned from the start, and even the most pious believers and ostentatiously good-hearted are painfully aware in the darkest corners of their minds that eventually they'll be left behind and the world will proceed forward without them. Through the centuries and over thousands of years, I've watched as the barely civilized and the advanced alike scratch and claw for any scrap of fiction that will allow them to believe salvation is theirs–that they are the wheat, not the chaff—but you can only pretend for so long, you can't ignore reality peering over your shoulder forever. Jill, when you saw Brad in his Tarzan costume you knew it was over – that the end hadn't been agreed upon or negotiated but that you had been simply left behind. You grabbed a comet by the tail and held on longer than you imagined possible, but you knew the day would come when the dazzling ball of fire would slip through your fingers and sail away. That's life—that's your life, that's everyone's life. Brad just reminds you that one day it will all end. You won't know who won an election or who was awarded the million-dollar prize on a reality show, you won't see the flowers bloom in the spring, hemlines rise and fall, or the next generation take flight and head off towards their own inevitable damnation without you.

Jill, I'd like to explain further how masquerade ensembles are just gaudy, glitzy versions of the guises people choose to wear every day, but I have my own Halloween costume to plan, so I'm afraid I have end here and leave you behind. Good luck…and I'll be looking for Tarzan.

MEMORIES OF FATHER TOM

Alexios,

I went to Catholic grammar school in the 70s. I graduated in 1978, and I haven't kept up with any of my old friends from school in years. I don't even live in the same city anymore. Two weeks ago an old classmate looked me up on Facebook and contacted me. He said that he had repressed memories of Father Tom molesting him numerous times, but now it's all come back to him. Paul said he has contacted others from school, and four of them have said that Father Tom had molested them, too. I told Paul nothing happened to me, but be he thinks I'm blocking the memories. I've been trying very hard to think of anything weird that might have happened, or to jog my memory, but I don't remember anything bad happening. One time Father Tom called me a hopeless case in front of the whole class when he handed out report cards, but I don't think that counts. I don't know why Paul and the others would lie. What should I do? I haven't even told my wife about this yet. Should I just tell him again that nothing happened? Or should I make up a story? Maybe I am blocking the memories.

Randy

Randy,

Memories most definitely love the corners of your mind, but they haven't been banished there, nor are they beating a hasty retreat; they like to make themselves comfortable, to settle in and take up permanent residence...especially the bad ones. The good memories of your mother will swirl together into one hazy Hallmark recollection, more idealized than distinct, but the pattern on the wallpaper behind the nursing home bed she died in will forever haunt you as a vision of stripes and tiny floral print rendered in razor sharp clarity. A long-past love affair will be remembered in gauzy abstraction, but the betrayal that ended it will remain with you – a silent but ever-present companion on your journey. A starlet who tumbles on the stairs when accepting her Academy Award will expend considerable effort in an attempt to wipe away the memory, but those several unbalanced seconds will play over and over in her mind like an endless tape loop. Tragedies, slights, and injustices propel a person's life forward — you need something to run from before you can take that first step towards what's next. If you feel happy and safe and content, you'll sputter out and stall in lazy repletion, but anxiety jolts you like a five-hour energy drink. More than three decades have passed since your parochial grammar school days, but Randy, you still recall Father Tom pointing you out as a "hopeless case" in front of your classmates, and that caustic memory has become a bloodthirsty tick burrowed under your skin. No doubt, you'd certainly remember if the priest had stuck his consecrated finger up your ass, but considering your lack of recollection, you probably weren't one of Father Tom's favorites.

Over my lengthy existence I've encounter a number of holy men, and I remember them all as con artists, creeps, greedy grifters, dodgy politicians, or rabidly ambitious self-promoters.

Many centuries ago, in the dreadful year of 1095, I was in the mood to make some mischief, so I devised a fantastic scheme to pit god against god, faith against faith in a holy war that would burn through the ages like an unquenchable grease fire, but I needed the powerful pontiff to set my plan in motion. And so, in the darkest hours of the night I paid a visit, like an apparition, to the dour Pope Urban II. The old man greeted my midnight appearance not with fear, but with a giddy sense of exaltation. He dropped to his knees before me, grabbed both my hands, then rose and lightly stroked my cheeks. I felt as though my personal space had been violated in a most inappropriate manner, but my initial impression was that Pope Urban had simply overreacted after mistaking me for the Almighty himself. Only when the Holy Father began to whisper suggestive and vulgar obscenities in my ear did I realize that I had entered the private chambers of a high-profile pervert. For the first time in thousands of years, I feared it might be necessary for me to step out of the smudgy shadows as history's agent-provocateur and into the spotlight, and as Urban patted me and murmured explicit sweet nothings, my mind raced with the various ways that I might assume the politically potent papal throne as my own. I even chose a name for myself: Pope Malfeasance I. But practicality, along with a sharp slap across the pontiff's infallible face and a vice-like grip wrapped around his throat, quickly returned my visit to its intended purpose. I sternly issued the cowering pope detailed instructions and a blunt warning of dire consequences should he fail to execute the directives to my lofty satisfaction. Only then did I release my stranglehold, leaving the nearly hysterical old man in a crumpled heap on the floor to crawl back into his bed and hide beneath the blankets. Soon after my unpleasant experience with the Pontifex Maximus, the savage First Crusade was unleashed, but even with my instigation of that towering event looming over my recollection of the proceedings, I still have not forgotten the clammy touch of the pope's trembling fingers on my face.

Randy, I think we can dismiss the notion that you were ever a youthful object of Father Tom's sordid affection, so I'm mystified by your inclination to fabricate an unholy dalliance with the parish priest. Are you looking to insinuate yourself into a lucrative payout, or are you still desperately battling the lacerating memories of being the last kid picked for dodge ball? Either way, creating a custom-tailored narrative that would place you squarely in the middle of the action is a dangerous gambit that could very well backfire in a most unpleasant way. How would you feel if the accusations against Father Tom moved through the legal system only to have your personal charges alone among the others dropped as unsubstantiated? Imagine your irredeemable humiliation if the aged priest was moved to seek an end-of-life redemption through a humbled, teary-eyed, publicly presented contrition for his sins against your classmates, then pointed to you and said, "Not that one, though. I never touched him." Randy, you're not struggling to acknowledge a ghastly episode from your past or attempting to drag a murky childhood trauma into the clear light of adulthood. The question isn't, "Why me?" but rather, "Why *not* me?" Rejection, not abomination, preys on your mind.

Rejection is a scalpel that cuts effortlessly through the skin and sinew all the way to the bone. It peels back your comfort and complacency and lays bare your self-doubt. "Thank you for your interest in the position we are seeking to fill, however," "I'm flattered, I really am, but you're not my type," "I don't think this is going to work, I'm sorry." "But," "however," "I'm sorry." Those innocuous little words can send you into a tailspin of paranoid dubiety. Randy, you should feel lucky that you managed to elude

Father Tom's clutches decades ago, but instead, the mere suggestion of rejection has thrown you into a frenzied state that makes you question every aspect of your life. When your high school sweetheart walked down the aisle in her fluffy white bridal gown, did she see her Prince Charming waiting at the altar, or was Prince Charming the guy on the wrestling team who screwed her like a stallion every day after class in the back seat of his Monte Carlo leaving you as the dumpy, dependable, safe alternative in a bad rented tux once the heady teenage years had evaporated into dull gray real life? Did your parents truly give preference to your older sister? And why were you passed over for a promotion last summer in favor of a younger, hipper co-worker? You feel no envy of your old classmate's sordid past, but Paul's stunning revelation stirred some painful memories of your own. Oh, you can pretend to push them aside, to block them out, to repress them and dismiss them, but you are your memories, and those psychological relics stand as monuments to a sad personal history. I wonder, does Father Tom looks back on his misdeeds with salacious gratification or if he's tormented by hideous demons in altar boy drag? Does Paul spend every day twisting in angry, victimized reflection?

Life is a cold, cruel ordeal with a few pin-points of pleasantness dotted along the way that offer up just enough hope to compel you to take one more breath, to face another day, to convince yourself that maybe tomorrow will be better. The here-and-now, the present, is a fleeting, momentary flash that becomes a memory in an instant, more often bad than good, and Randy, there's no point in torturing yourself with the pain of yesterday…tomorrow will probably be worse.

A PARENT'S HOMEMADE NIGHTMARE

Alexios,

My son Jacob graduated from college last spring and accepted a job with an advertising agency almost immediately. His father and I were hoping he would find a position in a large corporation, but he chose not to listen to his parents...again. He relocated to a city in a different state, so now we don't see him very often. He has come home to visit us for a week, and I went into his room to straighten up and accidentally noticed his laptop computer was still turned on. There was a file filled with pornography on his computer. It wasn't photographs, but little movies that didn't look professionally made, but were more like something home-made. One was of a man and a woman. Another had the same man with three women, in another he was with another man... and another was of him with two men. Then there was one of him alone using the cushions on an upholstered chair in a way that I would be too embarrassed to describe. I was so shocked by what I saw that I didn't realize right away that the man in all of the short movies was Jacob! As soon as my husband came home from work I told him what I had found, but he said that I was watching too many shows on HBO and was probably imaging strange things. We watched the movies on Jacob's computer together, and I viewed them again the next evening when our son went out with friends from school who we never liked. I am trying to figure out why he would do such a horrible thing. What should I do? I'm heartbroken and very disappointed.

Brenda

Brenda,

Homemade...the term conjures up cinnamon-scented memories of a sentimental time that exists only in the haze of imagination. It softens the sharp edges of reality with an artsy-craftsy quilt of denial, and "homemade" warms the frigid chill of production line mechanics when applied to the labels of canned soup and jarred pasta sauce. People bake homemade pies with prepared store-bought crusts and processed filling. It's a fiction, and in fact, there's more homemade crystal meth than homemade potpourri. Bombs strapped around the torsos of suicidal religious extremists are homemade, and domestic violence is another way of saying "homemade abuse." Homemade porn...the adjective ironically wipes a clean, damp cloth over the grime-encrusted noun, but the filthy images captured on cheap webcams and smart phones seem dirtier and more depressing than the high definition and color saturated product of professionally produced pornography. Porn performers are compensated for their services, and the adult entertainment industry provides them with a dubious job that might not read well on a resume but pays the bills nonetheless. However, the average person who bares their soullessness for free is driven by a personal compulsion that resides in a dark, shadowy place where monetary reward doesn't matter. Anthony Weiner sacrificed his political life when he was compelled to document the details of his anatomy reflected in a streaky bathroom mirror with his cell phone camera. Indeed, countless relationships and careers have been damaged or destroyed by a blurry image or a few minutes or seconds of furtive grunting and panting preserved on computer desktops, flash drives, and sleazy amateur websites. Brenda, your son Jacob certainly possesses a creatively open mind as well as a lack of shame, but I suspect motives stronger than an urge for exhibitionism led to the careless manner in which he left his little masterpieces exposed for you to see.

The relationship between mother and son is, on occasion, tragically complicated, to say the least, and both history and the arts have generously recorded the sad stories of those troubled bonds. From the start, the mother might set the narrative as easily as she pushes around her young son, but after the boy grows to be a vicious beast, the final chapter doesn't end well for momma. Brenda, you've joined the ranks of Jocasta, Agrippina, Eleanor Iselin, and Mrs. Gein. Don't try to trick an old trickster like me. You didn't go into your son's room to straighten up, and you didn't accidentally notice that his computer had been left on. I can understand a parent snooping through the personal belongings of a small child, but Jacob is an adult living his own life free from mom's prying eyes. What were you expecting to find, early Christmas presents? You wanted to discover some damning morsel that you could use to reclaim the power you lost when your son left his childhood – and you – behind, so you invaded his privacy. Brenda, you went fishing, and you hooked something very big and very unpleasant, and now you don't want the slimy creature thrashing and flopping around on your boat, but it's too late, and you'll suffer a nasty bite that will leave a scar when you throw that monster back into the murky depths. Your son is well aware that you've seen his handiwork. His computer wasn't left turned on by accident, and his exotic files weren't easily accessible as an oversight. He punished you with the graphic reminders of his fully adult status because you've probably always been intrusive, bossy, and demanding with a history of searching through his private possessions. Whether you care to admit it or not, you've been battling Jacob for control ever since he learned to use the bathroom by himself, and to finally win the long, drawn-out war, he brought out the heavy artillery: his homemade smut. I admire Jacob; he's a wicked young man, and not because he behaved wantonly with an assortment of individuals (as well as an upholstered chair) before the unflinching lens of a digital camera he bought at Best Buy. Your son understands people's naturally nasty instincts, he knows how to manipulate that unsavory reality to suit his own needs, and he knows winning is more often cruel than noble…he sounds like a lot of fun, too. Jacob's not evil like a genocidal despot or sadistic serial killer, but he is a heartless devil, and this is a heartless world.

The guillotine blade didn't rise and fall because I appealed to the noblest angels of the French people; I spoke directly to their inner demons. The Crusaders didn't march to the Levant after I stirred the righteous convictions of the faithful; I aimed carefully and hit the raw nerve of their deepest fears and hatreds, then sent them off like a savage plague to scourge everything in their frenzied path. Call me a monster, call me a fiend…sticks and stones may break my bones, but the truth will never hurt me. My work over the centuries has provided a graphic illustration of mankind's irresistible impulse to wallow in his own worst instincts, although war, revolution, and chaos aren't required to prove my point. Next time you hit the gas pedal so you can block another driver's fleeting opportunity to make a left turn, you just might find me smiling in your rear view mirror. Brenda, when you first glimpsed Jacob's image writhing and wriggling on his laptop's screen, the correct response should have been for you to claw your eyes out and then spend the remainder of your medi-cated, tortured days sequestered in a special place with attentive nurses and burly guards on duty 24 hours a day, but instead, you chose to watch your son's entire body of work…three times. The gravitational pull of depravity was too great for you to resist, and now you're attempting to mask your submission to the foulest of fascinations with a haughty air of indignity. Your race to the moral bottom was matched by your son's – and he was waiting in the depths to mock you. Guilt bedevils you, not the image of Jacob's "talent" burned into your mind.

A guilty conscience isn't a soul twisting in morally compro-mised turmoil and self-doubt over a misdeed or lapse in judg-ment; a guilty conscience is nothing more than anxiety over the possibility of getting caught. Brenda, you got caught. Besides, you can't "unsee" what you've already seen, and you'll never again be able to regard Jacob as just your son. Now he's someone you can't control, someone you don't understand, someone you don't really know…and it's your own fault. My only advice to you: In the future, mind your own damn business.

GOOD AND EVIL

Alexios,

I could never tell this to anyone. If I told my friends they would probably think I was a terrible person. If I told my husband he would probably leave me. I don't know if you can help me, but maybe you can at least understand what I'm feeling. I've been married for eight years to a great guy. We're both professionals and are very good at our jobs. I can't complain about anything because we have a very good life. We have a six-year-old daughter; Betheney is everything a parent would hope for, and we are truly blessed to have her. She's very smart and excels at everything she does…tumbling, ballet, etc. She loves to sing and is a natural little performer. She loves to put on a show for our friends whenever we entertain, and she's very popular with the other little children in the neighborhood…and I can't stand the sight of her. Other people see a talented little star, I see a little show-off. No one would ever guess how I feel, I act like the perfect mother. I feel so guilty.
Terri

Terri,

With their big heads, little bodies, and squeaky, wee voices, children are every bit as creepy as clowns, and I'll never fathom why priests find them so enchanting. Look carefully at any photograph of parents in the hospital with their newborn babies, and you'll see that mom and dad never look happy. Oh yes, they smile, but it's the sickly, queasy smile of an angler on a fishing vacation who's just discovered that there's a squirming eel on the end of his line, not a large-mouth bass. Modern society dictates the boundless adoration of children because kids are big business. We live in a child-based economy. The percentage of a normal household income that is devoted to the maintenance of the insufferable tykes is enormous, but it wasn't like that in by-gone ages. Children were viewed as barter in the joining of families, or as nothing more than another pair of hands to help with the day's work. I vividly recall that the Romans' utmost disdain for infants caused them to squeeze and mold their babies into restrictive garments that would force those shapeless little bodies into a more pleasing adult-like form. So Terri, you must understand, unconditional love and slavish devotion to offspring are not natural human traits. The whole thing is a commercial racket no different than a Christmas devised to sell gullible people everything from excessively elaborate toys to over-priced college tuition.

You don't feel remorse over your appropriate dislike of an unpleasant person; you feel guilty knowing that you are responsible for creating and encouraging a child who sings and dances like a miniature Josephine Baker even if no one in her vicinity expresses any desire to be entertained. Dr. Frankenstein had regrets too, and Terri, you are no different than literature's most famous misguided mad scientist. You are responsible for your own creation, and you are shackled to the care of Betheney right up until the moment she's squeezed the last dime out of you and then locks you away in a nursing home where you'll spend your final miserable years wondering how your life would have unfolded if only that goddamn condom hadn't broken so many years before. But you also bear the responsibility to ensure the monster you made doesn't offend *my* sensibilities.

Judging solely by the brief description you offered, I can emphatically assure you that I share the disdain you feel for Betheney, and I can say with confidence that the guests who visit your home for a cocktail party or backyard barbeque would rather not be subjected to your daughter's cabaret act. Terri, the root of your anxiety, the gnawing fear eating away at you, is the dread that your true feelings will rise to surface and that you'll be viewed in a manner described as less than "good." A widespread belief holds the notion that mankind has a free will to follow a personal path that leads to good or evil, and while I have no use for theology, I must in this case agree. Everyone must choose whether or not to act in a fashion that can be classified as either "good" or "bad," but altruism plays no part in the decision. Life is a never-ending struggle to take a step forward, climb higher, and attain a more advantageous position. Both "good" and "bad" are merely a means to an end. If Mother Theresa had been able to sing like Janis Joplin, do you think she would have wasted her time with the poor? In her limited circumstances all she had at her disposal was "goodness," and that propelled her to world-wide fame. Michael Jackson's prodigious charitable work masked the darker shadows hanging like a sooty cloud over his troubled personal life. The good deeds painted over the bad inclinations, and Jackson remained a beloved figure to millions of fans right up to moment he died of a professionally administered overdose in his Neverland house of horrors. After her decadent stardom fizzled away, Elizabeth Taylor recreated herself and found a second career as a saint. When the Devil tempted Jesus with the shining mirage in the desert, the Son of God didn't reject the offer as a show of righteousness. Practically speaking, the Devil's offer made no sense for the career trajectory the Messiah had mapped out for himself. Nearly two thousand years later, Bugsy Siegel saw infinitely greater possibilities in Satan's proposal, but a shimmering city floating in the desert heat naturally made much more sense to a man with neon lights, big box-office lounge acts, and mass transportation readily available. For iron-fisted despots like Joseph Stalin or Chairman Mao, "goodness" is unnecessary to grease the skids of success, but the President of the United States must wrap himself in a righteous mantle if he wants to become the most powerful man on earth. "Goodness got nothin' to do with it," Mae West famously said, but goodness has a whole lot to do with it as an option as potent as badness.

Life is selfish. Life swallows whole anything that can propel it forward, and it pushes aside anything that might hold it back. Years ago, when people had the distressing habit of wearing shoulder pads and their hair teased high, I went to a chamber music concert with my friend Sebastian, a vampire I first met when Charlemagne was on the throne. The concert, held in benefit of an AIDS organization, was pleasant but went on at least twenty minutes past what I considered to be comfortably tolerable, so it was a relief to finally leave the theater and go to the reception in the lobby that followed the performance. I was busy alerting Sebastian to the presence of a woman in the crowd who should have chosen her outfit more carefully when an unremarkable man in his late-thirties interrupted and introduced himself as Neil. Neither Sebastian nor I had time to react to the intrusion before Neil began to buffet us with a lengthy litany of his charitable endeavors. Two nights a week he delivered meals on wheels, another two nights he volunteered in the

AIDS ward of the county hospital. Teen mentoring, hospice care – Neil continued unabated as if a faucet of beneficence had been turned fully on. Sebastian, more a gentleman than myself, listened courteously with a somber expression on his chiseled, handsome face while I did some quick math in my head and figured that Neil's week must have two more days in it than mine. Eventually Neil paused for a breath, smiled the type of wan smile I've only seen displayed by the Virgin Mary on nicer Christmas cards, and sighed, "I've already lost twenty-eight close friends to AIDS." Sebastian lowered his eyes and nodded. "Twenty-eight?!" I gasped. "I'd have to lose strangers!" Painfully polite, Sebastian remained silent. There is only a subtle difference between panic and horror, but in a matter of several fleeting seconds I saw both emotions clearly take their turns dancing across Neil's pallid face before he backed away and disappeared into the chattering clusters of people gathered around one of the service bars. "Who has twenty-eight friends?" I asked, and Sebastian frowned slightly, then said, "Well, I suppose if I counted everyone up over the centuries." I tugged his sleeve and discreetly pointed across the room. Neil had cornered a well-dressed elderly woman with red lipstick and silver hair worn in a pixie cut, by a pastry table laid out with an assortment of sweets and small deserts. He held up a pair of fingers and waved them gently, so I assumed he was telling the old lady about the two nights a week he candy-striped, or maybe about the other two nights he volunteered on the safe-sex counseling bus. Neil was selfish. He didn't offer his time out of the genuine goodness of his heart. He craved admiration; he was an admiration parasite, and because he didn't have handsome looks, an engaging personality, or a clever wit, he relied on a manufactured aura of goodliness, generosity, and heartbroken devotion to attract admiring attention. We're all selfish, each in our own way, each to our own end, and both "good" and "bad" are equally available to meet our needs.

Terri, I don't suggest that you become openly hostile to your detestable young daughter, but you must accept – and embrace – your dislike of her. The situation will only become worse as the years roll by. She will transform from a miniature song-and-dance monster into a shrieking teenage harridan, and that nightmare will be followed by a young adult iteration of Betheney who smugly informs you that your taste in home furnishings or style of dress "...isn't my aesthetic." When you become a grandmother, your daughter will keep you at arm's length and sharply remind you of your failings as a parent during her own formative years. By embracing your aversion to this loathsome little creature, you will immunize yourself to the pain of the slights and slings and arrows she'll certainly send your way. I've always suspected that when confronted by the horror of a burning house, even the most devoted parent's natural immediate inclination would be to save their beloved pet before their child. Get a puppy. The adorable creature will return your devotion without hesitation, and that will allow you to view Betheney as just another unpleasant but necessary chore...like cleaning the bathroom. Terri, I can't say you're good a mother. In all likelihood, you probably could be considered a terrible mom, but good and bad are relative, so in the long run, does it really matter?

SWIMMING POOL ETIQUETTE

Alexios,

One of my buddies moved into an apartment complex with a big pool, so the group of us has been hanging out there on the weekends. The first time I went I had to battle a very strong urge to do something bad, but now for the last few weeks I haven't been able to keep it in check, and I've been urinating in the pool. I know I'll do it again. Should I stop going to my friend's pool?

Scotty

Scotty,

You're a pig. I mean no disrespect by that; after all, people are pigs...it's simply human nature. Ever since primitive man first wound decorative twigs in his matted, lice-infested hair, a species-wide effort has been employed to deny the true filthy constitution of the two-legged beast through painted-on pigments, splashed-on fragrances, and the wearing of adornments made from metals, shiny stones, natural fibers, and synthetic blends. Evolution has led us from wrapping ourselves in roughly-cured mastodon hides to wearing Giabattista Valli and Tom Ford, but the intent has been the same from the start: to mask the animal and embellish the man. Watering holes, public bathing areas, and swimming pools have always brought out the slimiest, dirtiest attributes that have clung tenaciously to mankind, going all the way back to the most ancient, mist-shrouded beginnings. Every living thing shares an ancestor that sprang from the primordial waters, and there's a natural inclination to revert back to those mindless prehistoric roots when immersed in the liquid of life. The Bible invented a sexy soap opera around the beheading of John the Baptist that involved a fictional princess and a lurid dance that was, in essence, a classic striptease, but historians explain the prophet's demise in a more mundane political manner. Prophets, messiahs, and miracle workers notoriously plagued Herod Antipas' domains, so the ruler simply eliminated a problem before it could spiral out of control, according to academics, but it was I who suggested the course of action for purely hygienic reasons to the Tetrarch. John submerged his throng of followers in water that was about as pristine as one of the toilets in a Yankee Stadium restroom. Believers would emerge from their baptism and exhibit symptoms of salvation that was often remarkably similar to dysentery. Famously fussy and fastidious, Herod followed my advice and gave his soldiers the order to, "Clean up that goddamn mess before we all end up sick!" Hardly as glitzy as the "Let Me Entertain You" fantasy of the Bible or as sonorous as the historical accounts, but from a purely practical point of view, my advice to Herod was spot on.

I'm dead. I have been for thousands of years, so you might assume that microbes and germs and viruses and their icky companions hold no offense to my sensibilities, but I carried my affinity for cleanliness from the realm of the living to that of the undead in a heightened manner that might be described as compulsive. Plagues, illnesses, and maladies both minor and major pose no danger for me, yet I can't abide filth, but as hard as I try to look the other way, I can't help but notice the unsavory and unsanitary everywhere. When summertime arrives, I spend more time than I care to admit noticing the dreadful condition of the feet many people happily expose in sandals. My attention is immediately diverted to anyone who even discreetly raises a finger to his nose. Last week an attractive and dapper gym acquaintance of mine, Jeremy, invited me to see a loud, special effects-laden movie about giant robots at an IMAX theater, so on a hot, humid, drizzly night we waited in a long line to buy tickets surrounded by sullen teenage fans in baggy tank tops and dingy shorts. Once inside the lobby I found a spot near the theater entrance to wait for Jeremy after he headed off to the concession stand. Left to my own devices, I began to obsess on the rain-dappled and disheveled condition of my fellow moviegoers, causing me to develop some serious concerns about my own appearance. I made a quick trip to the men's room so I could check myself in the mirror, but I was instead greeted by the horrifying sight of Jeremy standing at one of the urinals holding a Popsicle. People are pigs. It's human nature. Families lumber through street fairs chewing on dripping turkey legs and buttered ears of corn, only to wipe their greasy mouths with the backs of their hands like savages. I've seen smartly dressed diners at outdoor restaurants lick their fingers as they eat messy barbecue ribs and act as if every protocol of decent behavior has been scrupulously subscribed to simply because they're wearing expensive clothes from Saks or Barney's. Perfumes and colognes may now be used as aphrodisiacs or a statement of your high-priced taste, but originally they were intended to mask human stink. In all honesty, a white tablecloth is just about the only thing that separates humans from hogs at a trough.

Ironically, on the very night I witnessed Jeremy relieve himself with one hand while enjoying a frozen treat with the other, he told me of a fellow gym member who is routinely seen urinating in the locker room shower. People + water...well I'm beginning to believe the answer to that equation is clear. When Navy SEALs, in the midst of their arduous training, are tossed into a pool with their ankles and wrists bound, do you think they wriggle to the surface and ask to be excused should the need to visit the restroom arises? Esther Williams probably urinated in plenty of pools before her director called out, "Cut!" and Michael Phelps has pissed in pools all over the world. Public pools might shimmer with a crystal aqua brilliance, but whenever you dip your toe in, rest assured that you just wetted yourself with the urine of anyone who's jumped in and stirred about, and next time one of your friends dives in headfirst, watch him sputter and blow like a harpooned whale when he emerges in a viscous spray of his own sputum and phlegm. Many pools require babies to wear swim diapers at all times when in the water, but aside from a savvy marketing campaign designed to ease fellow bathers' minds, I doubt there's much difference between a swim diaper and a coffee filter. Next time you see the elderly enter the pool, remember their self-control is shaky at best. You're not swimming in your friend's pool every weekend, Scotty, you're splashing around in a fucking toilet.

Scotty, I'm somewhat confused by the nature of your letter. Is it merely a confessional? "Bless me, Alexios, for I have sinned"? Are you trying to expunge a pee stain from your conscience, or are you seeking peace of mind – an assurance from me that you've done no wrong? Maybe you feel a sense of guilt or remorse when you see your buddies swimming in your urine, but I think you're having a difficult time merging your modern mind with the primitive instinct to wallow in your own filth. Everyone is peeing and spitting, and worse, in that pool. You're just a member of the squalid tribe, part of the stinking herd. People are pigs…it's human nature. There is nothing you can do but accept it and embrace it, and before Labor Day rolls around to close down the fun, I want you to stand on the diving board and to openly and proudly piss in that pool.

AMORE

TRUE LOVE

Love. You love your children and your husband, too…but you also love pizza. Which do you love most? Who do you love more—your wife or your mistress? Or is your love of football greater than the affection you feel for either of the women complicating your life? John Lennon famously sang "All You Need Is Love," but like a supplemental insurance policy to augment what love couldn't provide, he had a vast fortune, worldwide fame, and a swanky co-op apartment in the Dakota. All you need is love if you don't have to wonder where your next meal is coming from or worry about the mole on your neck that's suddenly gone through an alarming transformation.

Love is a many-splendored thing; it's a drug, a battlefield…it makes the world go 'round, and it's blind. Throughout my travels over countless centuries I've noticed that only a few things remain constant as civilization shifts and changes and reinvents itself for each new age, and "love," despite its many guises, stands as one of the most durable, dependable, and all-consuming of quests, commodities, and concepts life has to offer. A few cheerful souls love life in general; others profess love for another until death do they part, while some people love certain breeds of dogs, particular colors, various types of food, or popular celebrities. Is there one singular "love," or is love like a man-o-war jellyfish: a toxic creature created from a multitude of distinct organisms? When the fevered flush of romantic loves does its quick fade, what remains behind; a deeper, more profound version of the emotion, or nothing more than complacency? Did an elite soldier who boasted that he loved to kill still love killing when the gun was pointed at himself? Was his "love" no different than another person's love of painting, singing, cats, or cultivating orchids? Love is a catchall term for anything you desire or anything that pleases you. It's a selfish, greedy, ravenous self-indulgence, not a notion to be exalted or cherished. The sum total of The Seven Deadly Sins equals "love." The carpenter from Galilee knew he had to appeal to his followers' naturally self-centered inclinations if he hoped to sell any of his heavenly time-shares, and so he preached, "Love thy neighbor as thyself." I don't believe love truly exists; it's nothing more than the whipped cream and cherry on top of a wish you know will never come true. Love is an excuse for bad behavior and the most craven and avaricious of impulses. It's by no accident one of the classic declarations of love is the grasping, clinging, demanding, and vaguely desperate, "Be Mine." Greeting card companies, florists, jewelers, restaurateurs, and the designers of undergarments are quick to say love is in the air to bolster sales of their wares. I can tell you something stinks, and just maybe it is true love.

Bits and pieces of sentences, fragments of phrases, names, and a few words here and there drifted back from the two girls walking several paces in front of me. As so often the case with friends, one was attractive and confident, moved with self-assured ease, and set the agenda for the relationship while the other was ungainly and homely and carried herself with uncomfortable, jittery envy. Judging by the scraps of conversation that reached me, I could tell the pretty girl, Emma, was complaining about her boyfriend, her job, or her mother. Although in the larger scheme of things it didn't matter who was the object of her scorn, as I had the distinct impression she lived in a chronic state of displeasure and disappointment with someone or another in her life. Suddenly, her big-boned companion, Mackenzie, interrupted by pointing to a little storefront restaurant and squealing, "I love that place!" Emma reacted with annoyed surprise and said, "What? There? Oh, I guess, yeah…anyway," then returned to her story. A moment later, Mackenzie pointed out another small eatery she loved as much as the previous one, and by the time I quickened my pace and passed the two friends, Mackenzie had expressed her heartfelt affection for three restaurants, a clothing boutique, and a small bookstore, all in the matter of a few disruptive minutes. Clearly, she loved Thai food and specialty cupcakes, but perhaps her rapid-fire effusion was a signal that she felt no love for her friend Emma. With the girls receding into the background, I approached a young couple walking hand-in-hand. A homeless man asked for some spare change, and the boyfriend half of the twosome announced, "What if he's Jesus?" "Huh?" his confused girlfriend responded absentmindedly. "That bum." The philosophical beau pointed to the homeless man and said too loudly to be considered courteous, "Maybe he's Jesus in disguise, and he's testing us." The young man smiled a goofy, crooked smile, quite satisfied with his own theological musing but oblivious to the fact that he had just failed his masquerading Messiah's test when he passed the unfortunate fellow without handing over a single dime. His girlfriend's gaze drifted across the street to a good-looking guy with a strident gait, square jaw, and a serious countenance. Where is the love, that junk emotion that people kill, die, and pine for so desperately? I wondered. A bus pulled up to the corner, and a handful of passengers disembarked, wincing at the sudden sharp slap of cold night air, and a burst of bright red caught my attention. Red, the color of passion, romance…and love.

The old woman was dressed from head to toe in vibrant candy apple red. She braced herself on the bus' hand rail and made her wobbly way to the curb, then paused to steady her wig – a champagne blonde version of Anne Miller's famous pitch-black flip slipping precariously forward and slightly to the left. Conversations gave way to gasps and snide asides as people watched the woman in her strange cape-like crimson coat teeter down the street – a walking bouquet of carnations in red pumps and a matching patent leather purse. She stopped in front of a coffee shop, checked her reflection in the window, then pulled the door open and stepped inside. I waited a moment or two, then followed her in. The barista, a twenty-something hipster with shaggy hair and in need of a shave, smirked to himself as he handed the old lady a cup of tea and a pastry on a small white cardboard plate, and the scattering of customers in the shop fell silent as the woman removed her coat and revealed a garment even more outrageous than her distinctive outerwear. The bright red dress was fitted at the waist and had a full skirt that fell several inches below her knees. Puffy shoulder caps led into tight fitting sleeves that opened up at the elbows into wide bell shapes that were edged, as was the hem of the skirt, in small, dangling red fuzzy balls, the type of decorative adornment often used to trim shower curtains in the 1950s and '60s. There were empty tables available, but I politely asked the old woman if I might join her. Eleanor smiled, flashed a set of snowy white dentures that were glaringly artificial when set against her wrinkled face, and said, "Oh! Of course you can!"

"You're very pale," Eleanor informed me as nothing more

than a simple observation, "just like the vampires in my TV programs, but those young men are always so handsome. You're... pointier looking." I answered her appraisal of my nosferatic nature and sharp features with the compliment, "That dress is quite striking...I've never seen anything like it before." "Thank you," Eleanor said, sounding as if she expected the admiration, "I made it myself, it's my signature look." "You must be a designer," I pressed on, hoping to flatter the old woman into an unguarded, talkative state, and with my words still hanging in the air, Eleanor indulged me and began to tell her story. "Oh no!" she laughed. "I worked for Westinghouse, on the assembly line, golly, for more years than I can count, so I wore a uniform, but I've always loved clothes, pretty clothes...ever since I was a small girl," she said. "My mother would get so angry," she continued, "I would cut apart all of her magazines, you know, tear out the pictures and the ads with all of the new styles, so she bought me a little sewing machine...that's how I started." Eleanor's life unfolded not through major events or milestones, but instead with a lovingly detailed description of each dress she had cobbled together. I quickly discovered that she had only mastered the construction of a single hopelessly dated design and had produced one identical frock after another in different fabrics and colors and prints over the decades. There were pastel versions that she would wear for Easter and on warm summer evenings, a floral print trimmed with fake flowers that she wore to her niece's graduation and then again to her neighbor's 25th wedding anniversary, a peacock blue dress with flapper fringe instead of the dangly fuzzy balls, and others in greens, golds, paisleys, and stripes. "Well, this beautiful red dress must be for a special occasion," I said, then I tried to coax something more personal out of her. "I'll bet you have romantic plans with your husband."

"My husband is dead," Eleanor said, taking a sip of her tea. "He died in the war...Vietnam, right at the beginning of it, he was one of the first." I suddenly realized this strange old woman, frozen in a bygone day like an insect trapped in amber, was just more wreckage that "true love" had dumped and left abandoned on the side of the road. "I'm sorry to hear that. You must still miss him very much," I said, using a tone of voice deftly balancing artificial sympathy with a gentle prod for more information. "Not really," Eleanor said matter-of-factly. She took a bite of her pastry, and a tiny snowstorm of powdered sugar fell onto the front of her dress. She carefully brushed herself off with a paper napkin and shrugged, "I don't remember that much about him. We were only married for two years, and it was all a very long time ago." She sipped her tea, and her face suddenly brightened. "I do recall the dress I made for his funeral," she smiled. "Of course it was black...beautiful black *crêpe de chine* with black lace trim. It was exquisite, one of my best. I only wore it once, you know, it was a special occasion and all." The old woman's blurry eyes focused on a spot somewhere between me and nothing, and she smiled and nodded, "I truly loved that dress," and for a brief moment I believed her.

I REMEMBER MOMMA

YoutTube is infested with countless videos of babies giggling rapturously as they touch, taste, hear, or smell something for the first time. Infants are mindless little beasts, parasites really, no different than leeches squirming in a swamp waiting to feed on a passing host, and their initial experience with grass or snow or Jell-O is nothing more than a primitive sensory response, so I've never been able to appreciate people's fascination with babies gurgling and bubbling and waving their tiny, fat arms after they've touched a terry cloth towel or a hairbrush. Eventually thoughts begin to form in those pint-sized brains, and "prickly" and "smooth," "wet" and "dry," "warm" and "cool" lose their enchantment…the child begins to understand the world instead of merely feeling it. My first memory, the first complex concept that settled into my mind as a profound revelation, was the cognition that my mother didn't like me. No words or actions expressed her dislike; it was the universally accepted expression of disappointment on her face every time she looked at me that resonated so strongly in my blossoming young mind. Don't expect me to whine or weep, to anguish over the sadness of it all, to write poems or spend hour upon hour dissecting the situation and examining its bits and pieces like a sample in a forensics lab. I don't like the color yellow, and my mother didn't like me. The situation doesn't need to be explained in terms any more complex or personal than that. I was a strong, healthy child, clever and resourceful, but in those ancient times when life was boiled down to its most brutishly basic elements, my mother could easily have cut me loose to devote her attentions towards the more favored members of her brood and no one would have thought poorly of her—and in all fairness to the woman, I wasn't viewed favorably by anyone in my family or clan. She tended to my needs and cared for me diligently, but the affection she showed to my brothers and sisters was completely lacking in our interactions, and as I matured into the independence of my teenage years, she chose to simply ignore me. Once I had reached adulthood we had, for all intent, parted ways. My mother was decrepit and ill, broken down by a harsh existence where every day was a battle for survival…simpler times, some say…when I mysteriously disappeared. I fell into the blackness and rose into an endless night that had no place or need for family and home, so I vanished. I left and never looked back. Seven thousand years later I think of my mother, my childhood, and that speck of time in the abstract. None of it matters.

The shopping mall was nearly empty as closing time approached. An elderly couple shook their heads and glared into the window of a clothing store that catered to the tastes of customers decades younger than themselves. "Jeez, are those things

supposed to be men or women?" the old man groused and pointed at the glossy white mannequins dressed in skintight jeans and
frozen in exaggerated poses that no real person would ever strike
– at least not in public. "Does it matter? They all look like…"
his wife began. Then she paused, looked around, then finished
her thought, "…whores." After shaming the mannequins with an
extended icy stare, the old couple turned their attention to the
young salesman standing idly behind the counter near the front
of the store's entrance. "Just like Nadine's grandson," the woman
whispered. "This country's goin' to hell," her husband answered,
and they moved on to buy some cookies at a kiosk before heading back home to watch a blood- and sex-drenched television
series on one of the premium cable stations.

I sat down on a bench to observe the last few shoppers who
wandered listlessly through the mall when I noticed two young
women seated beside a play area set up for small children. Both
women appeared to be in their early thirties, both were dressed
in a similar fashion, and each was the mother of a young son
who played on the low plastic slides and climbed on the large
padded blocks. The women might have been childhood friends
whose lives weaved side-by-side down the same road, or maybe
they were strangers whose paths simply converged in marriage
and motherhood and the playground of a shopping mall on this
one particular night. They chatted, swiveled their heads to check
on their children and then to check their cell phones. None of it
held my interest, so I prepared to go on my way when I noticed
something like a phantom hovering over the face of one of the
young mothers…a look of disappointment.

Where do people put the thoughts that they don't want to
acknowledge? Where do they hide the crushing truth about
themselves and the abhorrent feelings they harbor for those they
should love? Is there a steamer trunk that can be stuffed full,

slammed shut, locked, and pushed into a dark, dusty corner of the cellar? Oh, no. Life isn't so easy. All of that shit runs wild through your head while you're awake, asleep, every fucking minute it's there, and you can't shove it in a closet and pretend it's gone; it's who you are. The best you can do is to hold it all at arm's length and pretend that nothing is amiss.

Her face was impassive, nearly a blank except for the slight frown that settled on her eyes as she watched the two children play. They laughed and tumbled and rolled, one with more natural ease and a more engaging nature than his playmate, who possessed a vague quality that might be defined, for lack of a more specific term, as "different." "Settle down over there," the other mother called out to them as her companion sat still and silent, lost in a moment of terrible clarity. The woman's eyes moved from one child to the other, back and forth until she settled her gaze on the little boy who wasn't her own. She was tired after a long day, and the dreadful emotions, those terrible discernments that slunk around the corners of her consciousness like scavengers, scratched and clawed their way to the forefront of her thoughts. The woman wished she had a child like that one, like her friend's boy. He was what she'd always imagined when she dreamed of motherhood and a family of her own. Suddenly, she glanced down at her cell phone, rooted through her purse, then looked around uncomfortably and smiled at nothing in particular…forced distractions to deny the lacerating honesty that had overtaken her in a weary, unguarded moment. She loved her son, but the truth be told, she didn't like him. If I had walked up quietly like an angel of divine deliverance, laid a gentle hand on her shoulder, and whispered soothingly, reassuringly in her ear, "You can switch, you can trade, you can take the other one home," perhaps she would have clutched my pale, cold hand and looked up at me with tears of gratitude, tears of relief, brimming in her eyes, or maybe she would have just turned away in shame over the feelings that she didn't choose but couldn't ignore.

I walked through the mall with its vacant escalators silently moving, carrying no one from floor to floor. Everything – from the serene tropical plants to the composite marble appointments, quaint street lamp-style lighting, and fake cobblestone-paved walkways – was carefully devised to create a sense of comfort, of an ideal life that was proper and pleasant and as it should be, but life is much more complicated than that…and far from pleasant. I stood alone with Seals and Croft's "Summer Breeze" as a soft background hum hanging in the air, and I wondered what my mother would think if she knew me now, what she would say if she could see the dark creature that I became those countless lifetimes ago. I laughed to myself and remembered the look of disappointment. I paused for a moment at a small gift shop to browse through a rack of Mother's Day cards printed with color-ful flowers and sickly-sweet sentimental messages. Which card would I choose for my mother? On the bottom rung of the rack I noticed a card with a somber watercolor painting composed of overlapping muted-hued squares that decorated the front. The inscription inside the card read "For All You've Done for Me" … thank you for your hard work, in appreciation for a job well-do-ne – a businesslike endearment. I left the mall as the metal se-curity curtains began their rattling descent to seal off the stores until a new day began fresh. I stepped out into the night—my night. It felt good to be home.

CUPID AND COUPLES

An extravagant fairy tale wedding justifies its price tag only if daddy's little princess can walk down the aisle knowing her friends are bitterly jealous. That FTD teapot floral arrangement on your co-worker's desk isn't a tribute to her love; it's a loud and clear message in carnations and baby's breath telling you, "I have a boyfriend, and you don't." It doesn't matter that her boyfriend is fat and sweaty and screws plenty of other girls he meets when he goes out drinking with his friends; she has a boyfriend, and you don't...she is "loved," and you aren't. Love, romantic love—that most celebrated, idealized, coveted, and immortalized iteration of the shadowy emotion—is no different than a Jaguar parked on your driveway. Yes, it's unreliable, expensive to maintain, and troublesome, but it's a thing of beauty to behold and stirs the most envious of responses from your less fortunate neighbors. As hard as I might try, I can't escape the trappings of love at this time of year. Heart-shaped boxes of chocolates, flowers, syrupy greeting cards printed with the most sickly-sweet of sentiments are everywhere as Cupid's arrows fly, but trimmed of the lard, cut back to its simplest form, love is often a strange affair, more bewildering than mysterious, more confusing than captivating, and never really worth the trouble.

The other night I was in the mood for a movie, and, fortunately, several interesting and provocative films were being shown at an art house cinema in my neighborhood known for its foreign and obscure offerings, but as I was weighing the options and reading reviews I made the unexpected decision to head off for the nearest multiplex to see a movie about a comic book superhero in 3D. Shopping malls, supermarkets, and movie theaters are among the best places to view people in a natural setting stripped of any pretense, reduced to their most genuine unguarded element, and when I walked into the theater's teaming lobby I was immediately surrounded by sweatpants, mom jeans, obese people gorging themselves from enormous tubs of buttered popcorn, and children running about with a reckless abandon not expected to be seen in the civilized. Only a few gave much effort to putting-your-best-foot-forward or creating a presentable impression. I passed the video game arcades and large, freestanding die-cut promotional pieces advertising upcoming blockbusters and found the entrance to my movie. Standing against the wall next to the women's rest room was a young man with the type of good looks you usually see in models described as "all-American." His wavy hair fell over his forehead in a casual, easy manner, and he held his taught and toned frame in a way that was effortlessly self-assured. His serious face suddenly brightened with a broad smile as he pushed himself away from the wall and stepped forward to meet his girlfriend. I stood motionless, frozen in place as if some strange event had caused an imbalance or had knocked the world slightly off its axis. A short, flabby girl who looked frighteningly similar to Danny DeVito's Penguin character from *Batman Returns* waddled out of the ladies' room and took the handsome young man by his hand. He laughed happily and kissed her on the top of her head as she mumbled something of no importance or interest in a monotone voice – perhaps an amusing anecdote about her trip to the lavatory. Once I had taken a seat in the theater, I tried to forget the ghastly miscarriage of romance, but the disturbingly mismatched couple entered and sat directly in front of me. The girl laid her stringy, greasy head on her stunning boyfriend's shoulder, and they snuggled close together. I stood and politely excused my way down the length of the row and left the theater. I don't know why I felt so uneasy by the beauty-and-the-beast pairing, but I began to feel better as I hurried through the lobby and to the doors.

Before I was able to reach the street, my sensibilities were once again set reeling.

She was the definition of "pretty," with long, straight, dark brown hair, a trim figure, and flawlessly smooth skin. The young woman's partner was short and extremely skinny, and he had bizarrely large eyes set in a perfectly round head. His overall appearance suggested that of a recently-hatched snake. For a moment, I was tempted to ask the girl what unseen qualities this tiny young man with the receding chin and protruding Adam's apple possessed that would cause her to pass over more attractive prospects for romantic involvement, and I considered suggesting that she walk into Theater 6 and swap dates with Captain America and the Penguin, but in the end I felt it was none of my business.

Walking down the street, I came up behind an elderly married couple who had just come out of drugstore. They were the same height, the same weight, possessed the same shock of white hair, and even their clothes were nearly identical. He carried a plastic shopping bag in his left hand, she carried one in her right. They toddled back and forth in unison as they walked like mirror images of each other, and I wondered: at what point in their union did love strip them of their identities? When, in the name of love, did they cease to be individuals and become each only one half of a whole? Maybe the allure is beyond a creature like me, maybe the irresistible pull like gravity, like the tide, has no power over me, but for whatever reason, I'm no fan of love.

On my way home, I passed by the art house cinema and bought a ticket to a film that's a gritty adaptation of a Shakespeare play. Two middle-aged men took the seats next to mine and started a conversation with me, although I gave no signal that could have been misunderstood as friendly. They were nice, but dull in the manner that made me forget what they looked like the moment I turned my attention elsewhere. The two men had recently been married in a small, tasteful ceremony held in a tony restaurant owned by a chef who had gained a certain measure of fame through frequent appearances on a popular cable TV station dedicated to food and cooking. With no difficulty, I imagined them one day melting into a single featureless entity like the old man and woman I had seen with their plastic shopping bags and matching white hair.

I was relieved when the dimmed lights and movie ended our conversation, but Bobby and Frank walked out of the theater with me at the film's conclusion and invited me to join them for a drink at their favorite bar. The tavern was as average as Bobby and Frank; a large circular bar filled the center area of the main space, and to the right was an additional room with pool tables, dartboards, and a small service bar. The other patrons were all men as colorless as my companions. "No, thank you, I'm fine," I said politely at the bar when Frank offered to buy me a cocktail. "We've been together for fifteen years," Frank said, but Bobby laughed good-naturedly at his partner. "Sixteen—sixteen years, Frank. You never get it right!" The light dusting of silver around his temples and the fine lines that appeared around his eyes when he smiled made me think that it was probably time for Bobby to drop the "y" and adopt a more grown-up "Bob" or even "Robert."

I had fulfilled my courtesy to their invitation and was thinking of a way to make my exit when one of the bartenders picked up a microphone and announced, "Are you guys ready for Cliff?" to an enthusiastic outburst from the crowd. Cliff climbed on top of the bar wearing nothing but old white gym shoes and a tiny, bright magenta garment that disappeared completely up his behind while from the front it covered barely enough to ensure the safety of the bar's liquor license. He had a flawlessly chiseled body, but I guessed him to be around 45. I was beginning to say my goodbyes when Frank gasped, "Oh my God! Cliff!" In unison, Frank and Bobby breathlessly informed me that Cliff was their "favorite" and then proceeded to turn their backs on me and aimed their full attention towards the dancer lumbering on top of the bar. Frank and Bobby pushed and shoved each other to gain a more advantageous position as Cliff navigated with less grace than I expected around the gauntlet of half empty glasses and beer bottles and then squatted down in front of the two men. I watched the spectacle unfold with a view of Frank and Bobby's backs. Their shoulders quickly rose and fell, and their elbows flew up and out from their sides with a frantic urgency that made me wonder if they were performing an emergency appendectomy on the dancer who calmly accepted the attention with complete disinterest. Like baby birds in a nest determined to get more than their fair share of the worm, the couple battled each other for the precious few moments of Cliff's time as they shoved dollar bills, one after another after another, into the clingy pink material that barely concealed the glorious Holy Grail of the dancer's impressive anatomy. Cliff stood up and moved down the bar when Frank and Bobby had exhausted their supply of tip money, and the couple watched him move away with an eerily obvious sense of abandonment. There was no need for niceties, no excuses required to take my leave. I simply backed away and left the bar unnoticed.

Love is dangerous, love is destructive, love is a weight that drags you down and keeps you from reaching for more than a girl who looks like the Penguin. Love is a stifling prison cell that no amount of cash shoved down a spandex thong can ever release you from, and love is a parasite and thief that robs you of the only gift that life gives...one's self. Most of all, love is silly with its fluttering hearts, rapturous surrender, and promise of forever. I know "forever" better than anyone, and it's got nothing to do with love. Years ago a friend sent me the only Valentine's Day card I've ever received. On the front was a beautiful painting of Cupid with his curly blond head resting on his bow. Inside the card was blank, but my friend had written, "See, he's sleeping. That's our problem." Awake or asleep, I think Cupid knows better than to aim one of his arrows at a heart that doesn't exist. His effort would be wasted on me.

INFATUATION

I swooned. My vision momentarily blurred, and I felt the earth shift under my feet the first time I caught a glimpse of Gaius Julius Caesar. Don't believe the statues; Caesar wasn't an impressive physical specimen. He was small, thin, and balding, but he possessed a bearing of supreme confidence and an intensity of purpose that added considerable heft to his otherwise unimpressive form. By the time of our first meeting, Caesar was already headed for the history books. The general's military success guaranteed his name a supporting role in the story of Rome, but I would make him a legend. His ambition overwhelmed his deeds, and in his relentless drive I saw the possibility for something huge and terrible...the destruction of the great and noble Roman Republic. Despite the graft, corruption, and incessant intrigue, the Romans were proud of their constitutional government, and I was anxious to prove how easily the ideals of checks and balances could disappear into the ravenous maw of tyranny. Julius Caesar, with his towering sense of self, over-reaching ambition, and lust for power, would become the pen I would use to write the history of an empire. Even a man consumed by an over-inflated notion of his own purpose and ability might waiver when standing at the precipice of "no turning back," and as Caesar paused to consider the profound step I urged him to take, I had to give him a final gentle push across the Rubicon.

Julius Caesar didn't live to be king, but that wasn't my intention. Octavian rose as Augustus from the ashes of Caesar's civil war, and Rome was ruled by an almighty, all-powerful emperor right up to the day the barbarians crashed the party. I rarely meddle in world affairs these days; there's no point. In truth, I peaked with WWII, but now the opportunities and possibilities for an epic world-changing event like that have sunk in the murky confusion of a global economy. The world is listing like a dead ship on a stagnant sea with no direction, no definition, and no individual viewpoints to chart new courses. Caesar wanted the world; Osama bin Laden was just a spoiled rich brat with a religious chip on his shoulder. Today, power is simply a means to a self-indulgent end, no longer a goal in and of itself. The objective is wealth and fame—preferably both, but either, alone, will do. Gone are the big, grand ideas, replaced by a variety of Ponzi schemes and dreams of show business relevance. There are no modern-day Julius Caesars. Caesar has been replaced with smarmy snake oil salesmen looking to fleece the gullible and line the pockets of their wealthy benefactors in hopes that a few crumbs will be thrown their own way. You see, that's the problem: nowadays, people are satisfied with crumbs. Some people expect more crumbs than others – CEOs and hedge fund managers demand a lot more than you – but no one really eyes the whole kit-and-caboodle anymore. No one sees beyond their own selfishness. The world has become a small, petty place.

I can't recall the precise moment. No thunderbolt hit me out of the blue; I didn't experience a Pentecostal awakening, but I felt as if I had opened the laminated cardboard door on the old Milton Bradley game Mystery Date and found Congressman Paul Ryan waiting for me in a white dinner jacket. At first I tried to rationalize the giddiness I felt. Perhaps I detected a bit of Caesar in the rascal from Wisconsin, or maybe I saw in the lanky lug a whisper of Wilhelm II, but when I began to diligently drag pictures of Rep. Ryan off of the *Huffington Post* and into a special folder labeled "Paul" that I had created on my computer's desktop, I realized my feelings were not steeped in the desire to find a vehicle that might steer an unsuspecting world towards chaos. Paul Ryan's swarthy good looks, five o'clock shadow, and buggy blue eyes captivated me, and his big nose and hands sent my imagination reeling. Over the ages I've been viewed in somber, serious, and dreadful terms. I've never been called "Mr. Happy-Go-Lucky" or the life of the party, and I've never led a pub full of hale and hearty merrymakers in a robust song or danced the Macarena, so panic began to set in as I feared that I might have begun to grow soft and squishy. A creeping horror settled about me as I came to terms with the terrible, unavoidable reality that I was infatuated. There was no point in resisting; I was powerless, and I began to watch cable news shows for a scant minute or two of Paul pontificating on my TV screen. I ignored the obvious fact that Ryan is a big dope with juvenile taste in literature, and I pretended not to notice when he was forced to flee a jeering crowd at his hometown Labor Day parade. Dashing to his car, the congressman struggled with his seat belt, then sped away in a spray of gravel and humiliation. Regardless of the ignoble display, I still wrote a poem about him.

Never before had I reason to shop in an arts and crafts superstore until I decided to make a decoupage wooden box decorated with pictures of Congressman Ryan. With a list of supplies in hand, I made my way to Michaels and stopped the first sales associate I saw to ask for some tips and advice, but he curtly informed me that he worked in "framing" and left me on my own, so off into the fluorescent-lit jungle of silk flowers and yarns and beads I marched. While searching the store for brushes and glue and colored papers, I spied a middle-aged woman holding an infant. Naturally, I assumed the tot was her grandchild, but her behavior was far more motherly than grandmotherly, and recalling the story of old Saint Elizabeth and her famous change-of-life baby, John the Baptist, my opinion shifted, and I decided that it was in fact a mother and child. The woman lovingly jostled and patted and cooed at the tiny bundle nestled in her arms as several other female shoppers smiled precious smiles and tugged gingerly at the little blanket. I've never appreciated people's fascination with babies or children, so I moved on and asked a sales girl who was checking price tags on a display of iron-on crystals and glitter thread where the sheets of gold leaf might be. A short, stocky fireplug with a whisper of a moustache, she pointed in a sweeping, ill-defined direction without otherwise acknowledging me. Eventually I found the gold leaf foil, and I picked up some extra-long pipe cleaners as well, even though I didn't need them for my project, then began to make my way to the check-out lanes at the front of the store. Once again I saw the middle-aged woman and her baby. She rocked the child back and forth for a new audience of enchanted ladies, but something seemed amiss, so I feigned a sudden interest in Styrofoam wreath-forms and worked my way closer. The old woman cradled a disturbingly authentic newborn baby doll as if it were a real living, breathing infant. As I stepped up next to her she turned, smiled radiantly, and carefully adjusted her arms so I could get a better look. I smiled and laughed, "Oh! That's not a *real* baby!"

The echo of a life-like vinyl doll head hitting the floor is a lonely sound. There is quiet, there is silence, and then there is the profound stillness that accompanies death. Something died in that moment, in that store – something that could never be picked up off of the floor and wrapped back in its blanket, something that could never come back to life in a tormented mind. I suspect a dead child haunts the strange woman's life, so perhaps I did her a favor. Perhaps I freed her from a past that cruelly stopped her life from moving forward, but I doubt it. Most likely she'll find something else to cling desperately to – another substitute that shields her from facing what needs to be done. Maybe she'll find her own Paul Ryan.

I retraced my steps through the store and returned the decoupage supplies, each to their proper shelf. Once back home, I turned on my computer and dragged the folder labeled "Paul" into the trash. In an instant, gone were the close-ups of Paul Ryan both smiling and scowling, gone were the pictures of him in his blue suit and others of him wearing khaki pants. I even deleted the weirdly unflattering workout photos he posed for that exposed his unpleasant vanity and hubris for all to see like Dorian with no place to hide the painting. We all cling to something at some point in our lives – whether out of weariness, boredom, disillusionment, or heartbreak, it doesn't matter as long as we stop life dead in its tracks. Many people, maybe most, can't let go once they've found an anchor, but I've never been one to stand still, and eternity is too long for me to hover uselessly in place. I think I'll do some traveling, get myself back out into the world again. Syria. I haven't been to Syria in centuries...maybe Ukraine. The possibilities are endless.

HOLIDAYS

DEATH AND CHRISTMAS EVE

History doesn't acknowledge Clyde Barrow and Bonnie Parker for their low-grade Depression-era outlaw antics. The criminal couple is remembered for their flamboyant jiggling and jumping deaths in a barrage of bullets. James Dean is a legend not because he left behind a few mumbling movie performances, but because he crashed into oblivion in grand style at the full flower of his youthful fame. Most leave-takings are far less spectacular and seldom memorable, and it's the routine, garden variety of death that inspires terror, not awe...terror of a bland finish to a dull life, terror of a humiliating finale wracked with pain and wrapped in soiled linen. When, where, and how? People probably ponder the notion of their own demise more than they fantasize about being a sports hero or a famous model, or dream of possessing a partner with stunning attractiveness, ferocious loyalty, and no unpleasant habits, but unlike those musings so blissfully free of anxiety and fear, angst clouds every thought of the end. When death comes, will it be heroic, epic in its tragedy, or luminously peaceful? At least that's what you hope for to balm the dread constantly burning like an infection. In your darkest thoughts you worry that death will visit in the guise of a lingering illness, a slow decent into senility, or as poverty and ruin, so you dress up the ugly images with weeping loved ones waving you off with white handkerchiefs or fantasize about a dramatic outpouring of public sorrow. I doubt many people would ever imagine the end…all alone, flat on their back in the pickle aisle of a nearly deserted supermarket late in the evening on Christmas Eve.

All alone…the shame of it. The Unabomber was a loner, and Garbo was considered odd when she announced, "I want to be alone," then disappeared into self-imposed obscurity. Home alone offers you no alibi; alone on Saturday night is a stinging sign of rejection; all alone in the world is a sad failure. "Solitude" gives some gravitas to "alone," but even so, it carries the pompous whiff of prickly indifference or contrived affectation. I prize my self-righteous solitude. I like to be alone, but I've never been one to apply socially dictated norms and expectations to myself. When I'm alone, my mind can race freely from one thought to another, from a half-baked concept to a meticulously considered deliberation, then fall just as easily into a gentle, restful state. Left to my own devices, I can watch professional wrestling on TV for three hours straight or revisit one of the classics of literature, depending on my prevailing mood. I enjoy my own company and laugh at my own jokes. For most folks, though, too much time alone is a penalty box, something you're sentenced to. Prisoners locked in solitary confinement for extended periods sometimes go squirrely and smear the cell walls with their own feces, but many people whose lives slip into a state of loneliness accept their fate with quiet aplomb. The shame is external. The shame gathers and congeals in your mind when you witness the seclusion of others, and it feeds the fear that one day, for reasons impossible to understand, you may find yourself like the woman ordering a single slice of pizza on her way home from work, like the guy sitting alone at a concert, or worse...taking the final bow to an empty house.

Last year on Christmas Eve I passed by a supermarket and was surprised to notice that it was still open, so I went inside to discover who might be shopping that late in the evening of such a cherished holiday. The store was empty save for the manager trying to look busy behind the customer service desk and two cashiers gossiping about a co-worker who was fortunate enough to be home. I could tell the store was preparing to close because both of the sullen workers graced me with sour looks that I acknowledged with an insincere, "Happy holidays!" At first I thought that I was the sole patron prowling the empty aisles, but then a young couple dressed for a celebration emerged from the liquor department with a bottle of Absolut vodka and a jug of wine that was too big to be any good. They passed me and disappeared down another aisle, and only a moment later I heard a scream. Actually, I heard the young woman screech, "Oh my God!" and her companion shout, "Help—someone help!" An old man was lying in the pickle aisle, his glassy eyes staring straight up, his face frozen in the last expression of shock before death had suddenly knocked him off his feet. The young man bounced from side to side as if he were doing a strange little dance while he continued to call for help, but the old man was past the point of any assistance. In all likelihood, the elderly gentleman would have made no more than a quick, blurred-around-the-edges impression on me if he had been alive, but dead in this peculiar circumstance, his personal details came into sharper focus. He was dressed neatly but casually in a pair of dark green sweat pants, tan boots, and a navy blue coat similar to what you would buy from Land's End but could probably be found cheaper at Target. His gloves were on the floor near the red plastic shopping basket that had held his groceries, which were now scattered about. A frozen rising-crust pizza, a zucchini squash, some type of roll in a plastic bag, a can of soup, and box of Oreo Cream cookies spilled out of the overturned basket. Near the man's gloves were two DVDs that he must have gotten from the rental box at the entrance to the store – one a comedy with several popular stars that did moderately well at the box office, the other an action science-fiction blockbuster. A meal for one and two movies – his Christmas Eve laid out for all to see on the linoleum. The store manager rushed down the aisle calling out, "Stay back, stay back!" even though neither I nor the young couple were standing very close to the dead man. "Did he fall? Did he slip? Did anyone see what happened?" The words shot out of the manager like bullets as he frantically dialed 9-1-1 on his cell phone.

The ambulance arrived more quickly than I thought possible, but once the paramedics entered the pickle aisle, their urgency faded away. One of the EMTs started to write on a form attached to a metal clipboard while the other two squatted down and began to lift the old man from the floor, and for just an instant he looked like the Pieta. They picked him up with great care and respect and gently laid him on the gurney, and in the end, the old man wasn't alone on Christmas Eve after all. It took only a few seconds for the paramedics to lift him from the floor and place him on the sheets, but in that fleeting moment the dead man shared something with them that might not be described in terms of family or friendship – maybe there isn't even a word for it – but it was a connection, profound and close. A pause between incessant carols left the store silent and still except for the quiet hum of a refrigerated display holding fruit juices and flavored teas. "We're done here," one of the paramedics said into his crackling walkie-talkie, and we were done. I made my way out of the pickle aisle and left the store.

Stepping back into the night came as a relief. I was glad to be out of the supermarket, away from the harsh fluorescent lights that don't flatter my pale white skin, away from the claustrophobic din of Christmas music that seeped into every space like a fog, away from the old man being wheeled out by the paramedics with the manager trailing fitfully behind, and away from the young couple who were paying for their liquor as if nothing out of the ordinary had happened. Life moves quickly to fill the void left by death. After my death I moved on, left everything behind, and began a whole new existence…a vampiric eternity that will linger on long after this time and place has faded away like some relic from a misty remote age.

I walked down a side street and passed by the apartment buildings that were like a checkerboard of light and dark. Some people had left their homes black and empty when they went to visit family or friends, others hosted festive parties behind their brightly illuminated windows. I stopped midway down the block and noticed a single window dimly lit. "The old man's apartment," I thought – an indulgence of my imagination. The sound of muffled laughter, of music and people in celebration, distracted me. I looked around, but the muted noise came from one direction, then another, from one building, then another, from this apartment, then that. I turned back to the silent, lonely little window. I'm a cold-hearted creature, but I felt bad that the old man would never get to watch his movies.

NOTHING MERRY ABOUT IT

I avoid Christmas as much as possible, but even a creature of my slippery talents sometimes becomes entangled in a situation that involves the exchange of gifts. "'Tis better to give than to receive," the old saying goes, and I must agree, not due to generosity of spirit or a good heart, but because I can tell you firsthand that there is nothing worse than receiving a fiber optic lamp with a big, bushy spray of thin, translucent strands glowing in a shifting rainbow of colored light. The gifts I give are carefully chosen to reflect my impeccable level of taste, and for my effort I receive in return a book with yellowed pages and obvious stains. Where is the joy in that? I'm convinced that there's a vindictive quality to the gifts many people give: gift as weapon, gift as insult, gift as passive-aggressive manifestation of the jealousies and resentments festering deep in a bitter soul. People see a festively-wrapped package with their name neatly written on a tag dusted with glitter, and hope is immediately polluted with dread. Visions of something coveted, something thoughtful, something exciting fill your heart, but lurking in the shadows of your more practical mind is the realization that behind the foil paper and bow is a cruel and insensitive reminder of life's endless disappointment.

Ironically, a holiday so steeped in anxiety is always described by words like "merry," "joyful," "wondrous," and "happy." There's nothing merry about Christmas – not its dismal carols dressed up with cloying jingle bells, not its drab red and green color scheme, and certainly not its cherished origin story. The Nativity, that O Holy Night, is a concoction cobbled together from old fables, tired prophesies, once-popular spiritual fads, and just plain fictional necessity. The concept of a virgin birth was not uncommon in those ancient times, although such an entrance into the world was normally reserved for major celebrities like Alexander the Great and Julius Caesar, not babies born in stables. The impossible biological feat was considered a great symbolic honor that no one was expected to actually believe. Christians, however, regard the story of Mary's immaculate conception with profound and somber piety, but the Almighty slinking down from heaven to bang a teenager is about as creepy as Jerry Sandusky in the shower at the Lasch Football Building, and it's hardly an original idea. How many half-god bastards did Zeus sire before he went into comfortable retirement as a museum attraction and star of corny special effects-laden movies? The Nativity story was intended to establish Jesus as the Son of God while fulfilling the Messiah's prophesied link to the lineage of King David, but divine plus royal isn't an equation that's very accessible to the unwashed masses, so the Galilean's birth was scripted in a manner to present his beginnings as "humble." Humble?! How about horrible? Admittedly, I'm a snob, I appreciate the finer things in life, and I avoid cheapness and vulgarity, so naturally I'm not attracted to barns—or babies, for that matter. Childbirth, even in a sanitary, modern hospital setting is a messy affair, but place the event in a stable two thousand years ago, and the Christ Child probably resembled a Baby Jesus Chia Pet with the ponderous amount of hay that must have been stuck to his slimy little newborn body. The livestock, the dirt, the stinking shepherds…thankfully the wise men showed up to lend a little sparkle and pizzazz, although St. Joseph, no doubt, looked at their extravagant gifts and wondered why the wealthy threesome hadn't brought something useful like Pampers or a car seat instead. Gold, frankincense, and myrrh…the fabulous magi didn't re-gift or go cheap, but myrrh is a spice used in embalming, so its appearance served as a chilling reminder of the Savior's brutal and bloody fate. The Passion hangs over the manger like a dark cloud that even the Star of David can't penetrate, and despite festive crèches and angels and little drummer boys, the Nativity story is at heart a dark fable… and I haven't even mentioned the Massacre of the Innocents.

From *A Christmas Carol* to *A Charlie Brown Christmas* to *Rudolph the Red-Nosed Reindeer*, the enduring holiday classics aren't nearly as heartwarming as most people's hearts wish them to be. Ebenezer Scrooge may have undergone an epiphany that transformed him from cold miser to harmless senile old fool in Dickens' tale, but after the final page has been turned, his newfound giddiness would never be able to make the dismal world that surrounded him any less squalid or cripplingly unfair. Every year, to the delight of millions, Charlie Brown mopes through his beloved Christmas special, and no one stops to worry why a boy so young should be so chronically depressed. I suspect there's a very good reason why we're never shown his home life, and Charlie Brown probably required a visit from Child Services, or maybe a good prescription, more than he needed Linus reciting the Gospel According to Luke. If retold today, would Rudolph the Red-Nosed Reindeer's beleaguered elf, Hermey, post a cryptic message on Facebook before hanging himself in Santa's workshop rather than endure another day of torture and ridicule at the hands of the tiny, pointy-eared bullies surrounding him? Would Rudolph show up at reindeer school armed with a black market semiautomatic Glock 19 and turn the snow red with Dancer's and Prancer's blood? "Even among misfits, you're misfits!" Yukon Cornelius callously tells Rudolph and Hermey, and misfits they remain. "Let them hate me as long as they fear me," the mad emperor Caligula famously said, and the red-nosed reindeer and his little elf friend could just as easily have proclaimed, "Let them hate us as long as they need us." There was no change of heart, no real acceptance at the story's conclusion. Don't fool yourself; Rudolph and Hermey became useful – necessary, not liked, not embraced. After torturing Whoville for ages, the evil Grinch experienced his own Scrooge-like Christmas conversion in the climax to *How the Grinch Stole Christmas*, but would you trust him? If John Wayne Gacy had claimed a miraculous transformation and said, "Come on, guys, let's build a deck!" should all have been forgiven? These cherished Christmas tales take life's dark, disturbing elements and paper them over with bright, simple colors, but the ugly issues remain, just momentarily hidden like an Old Spice gift set wrapped up and waiting under the tree.

Holidays have been with us ever since man first cowered from bolts of lightning, witnessed flowers spread open theirs buds, contemplated the tide, and waited patiently for the seasons to change. There has always been some deity to genuflect to in thanks for good fortune, a demon to appease to ward off calamity, some sprite or spirit to honor for nature's wonders, but no matter what the reason or who the honoree, holidays have always been celebrated with a guiltless over-indulgence of eating, drinking, and cavorting. Christmas is no different, and it has simply evolved into the biggest, most ravenous holiday of all – the Tyrannosaurus Rex of celebrations. Older folks like to remind their grandchildren of an earlier day when they didn't receive pricey cell phones or flat screen TVs for Christmas. They'd find an Etch A Sketch and a new pair of school shoes waiting for them on Christmas morning, but everything is relative, and yesterday's Etch A Sketch is today's iPad if you stop and think about it.

There was no Christmas when I was a boy; there was no Etch A Sketch or much of anything – even our gods were ill-defined murky concepts, centuries away from evolving into the tawdry celebrities living large on Olympus. Seven thousand years ago, there were no stately columns or sage philosophers, no Zeus, no brave Apollo. In the hinterlands we were nothing more than loose tribes just learning to farm and keep sheep corralled behind rudimentary fences. I lived in a small, crude house with my family, but I had a group of abhorrent relatives who still lived in a cave that could be compared to a modern-day trailer park. Mortified by their lowly living arrangements and boorish behavior, we tried to avoid them as much as possible, but even back then we had our holidays, so at least once or twice a year we were required to hobnob with our less-than-desirable kin.

My memory is like a steel trap; I don't forget anything, but some things, like my earliest years, I've deliberately covered with a thin, cloudy veil, and although I've blurred their reasons and purpose, I can't quite put aside the vivid memories of the holidays and festivals that I so hated. The big day would approach with a great anticipation and excitement that eluded my understanding. Everyone would dress in their finest garb, hostilities and bloodshed would cease just for a short while, and my family would gather with our various relations and neighboring clans for a festival of feasting, singing, dancing, and the usual activities that I always found more than a little embarrassing. My mother's youngest sister had entered into a family that held an area of land much larger than ours, and their house – still nothing more than a lopsided basic four-wall structure – was quite a bit nicer than what I lived in. We would be treated to a detailed account of the lushness of their crops, the abundance of their animals, the spaciousness of their abode, and the finery of their pots and vessels. My father would tense up and walk away; my mother would smile a stretched, strained smile and ask her sister if she was expecting another child even though it was clear that my aunt had simply grown stout. Eventually, the cave-dwelling side of my family would arrive late and loud, and their younger members would run about like beasts that had just been released from a cage. One of their menfolk who was fairly advanced in age routinely subjected most of the females young enough to be girls but too old to be children to leering looks and suggestive remarks, resulting in warnings and stern words from an assortment of fathers and mothers. I felt trapped amongst towering adults who frightened me and loathsome children I wanted nothing to do with, so I would find myself a quiet place to stand unnoticed until it was time to leave. Something would break, a child would fall, there would be crying, finger-pointing, and blaming cast in every direction, and all of the old jealousies and resentments simmering beneath the day's merriment would boil over. As night fell, the holiday would conclude in usual fashion, with no one speaking to each other.

As we journeyed home, my mother would grab me by the arm and demand to know why I had stood silent like a little mute boy. "People will think there's something wrong with you!" she'd say. My mother spent a great deal of time with worried thoughts of people believing there was something not quite right about me, whether for my lack of personality or for the art projects that I busied myself with. "Next time talk to people, play with the other kids." Then, releasing my arm, she would abandon me directly into my father's path, and he would roughly shove me out of his way without a word so that he could point out some feature of the landscape to my brothers. I would trail behind them – my mother and sisters gossiping about the other women of the family, my father and brothers involved in some deep discussion – and as the sky turned from deep inky blue to pitch black, I'd wish that I could melt away into the dark. Shortly after reaching my adulthood, that wish was granted in a fashion my young mind could never have imagined possible. The old holidays that I so dreaded as a child disappeared in time, replaced by others, which were eventually transformed and repurposed into festivals and holy days to suit new needs. I've seen all sorts of holidays rise and fall, shine bright, and then fade to murky obscurity before being forgotten altogether. I've outlasted all of them, and I'll outlast Christmas, too.

So go ahead. Have yourself a merry little Christmas now…

Last week I went shopping to buy myself a nice, expensive white shirt. Three young women dressed for a party cried out to me, "Merry Christmas!" and laughed as I stood looking in the window of a pricey department store. I turned and stared back at them with cold, black eyes that had no trace of holiday sparkle but instead held the grim reality of a world that's mean and hopeless. Their smiles disappeared as if they'd seen a ghost.

If they only knew.

Once in the store, I navigated my way through the crowd of shoppers, the cologne sprayers, and the numbing Christmas songs and found my shirt in the men's department. Richard was my sales associate, and given his striking good looks, he was far more friendly and helpful than I expected. "It's a beautiful shirt, really classic," he said enthusiastically as he wrapped my purchase in crisp sheets of tissue. Then he looked up and smiled, "It's a very nice gift." "It's not a gift," I corrected him. He hesitated for a second or two, then simply said, "Oh." When he finished carefully folding the thin paper around my shirt, he fastened the sheets with one of the store's gold stickers, laid the shirt in a glossy box, and wrapped a wide length of red satin ribbon around it, tying the ends into a big bow. He handed me my gift-wrapped shirt, smiled, and said, "Happy holidays!"

COMING DOWN
A CHIMNEY NEAR YOU

Even empty, the blood red and gold throne commanded the rapt attention of the anxious faithful waiting their turn for a few seconds in the blessed presence of the exalted figure soon to ascend the heights and take his place on the crimson seat. "Jesus Christ! How much longer?!" a frazzled woman with a set of unruly twins screeched, at the mall security guard who was wearing a headset on his ear and a bulletproof vest under his navy blue blazer. The line of parents and children wrapped around the kiosks selling junk jewelry and sunglasses, past Forever 21, and nearly to Victoria's Secret. I studied the young faces – fretful, needy, and starved for the attention of a beloved legend who offered a vision of life that was candy-coated with a sweet fiction far removed from the bitter reality of the drab real world. An adjustment was in order, a no-nonsense lesson. My eye returned to the throne, the hint of a smile brightened my typically-expressionless face, and I asked the security guard, "Where is the office?" "The mall office? Over there," he said, pointing to a set of doors discreetly tucked next to a showroom that sold cheap furniture. "Who's in charge?" I asked. "The whole place? Maureen, I guess. Maureen Dolan." The guard looked at his watch and wearily said, "She's still here. It's the holidays."

Maureen began her retail career behind the Le Metier De Beauté counter at Lord and Taylor. She moved on several years later to sell pricey dresses in one of the designer boutiques at Neiman Marcus before stepping down from the glitzy, rarefied world of the well-to-do to step up to a manager's job at Gap where she was charged with corralling a roster of lackadaisical junior sales associates. Older, jowlier, less inclined to smile helpfully, Maureen saw her years of hard work finally pay off with a position as Director of Special Events at a large shopping mall anchored by Macy's and Target. "Sorry, we don't need any more Santas. We lined everyone up a few weeks ago," she informed me sourly after I had inquired about the possibility of donning the red suit. "I don't even know why I'm talking to you. I don't hire the Santas," she said, all but ignoring me as she checked her emails. "I was given your name…" I began to explain, but Maureen abruptly silenced me, glanced away from her computer screen, and graced me with one of the most unfriendly grins I had experienced in quite some time. "Well I guess I'll just have to find out who gave you my name," she said, not so much to me, but more as a note to herself. As she typed a reply to an irksome message, Maureen fired off one last shot in my direction. "Anyway, we would never hire someone like you," she said with a good measure of barbed satisfaction. "Too young, too skinny…and, to be perfectly honest, you've got a mean look about you." She stopped typing and addressed me personally. "Kids want Santa to look like…Santa, not Count Dracula. We don't want to deliberately scare them." Maureen was beginning to cut a little too close to the bone for my comfort, but I remained seated calmly on the small chair upholstered in the type of striped fabric you only see decorating an office or nursing home. A knock on the door halted Maureen before she could tell me that I had eyes like the devil, and in stepped a timid young woman with long, straight, overly processed hair that badly needed urgent treatment at one of those salons where the stylists are all young and handsome and wear tight black t-shirts. "What is it, Heather?" Maureen snapped, and the young assistant winced slightly, then stammered, "Ed just called in sick." Maureen rolled her eyes and sighed, "Then call Don. Get him in here now, it's already late… for Christ's sakes, do I have to tell you how to do everything?" "He can't, not tonight. I already called him," Heather said, inching slightly away and protecting herself from the older woman with the office door. Maureen grimaced, then turned towards me and smirked, "Okay…so do you want to be Santa for a night?"

The red faux-velvet suit was ludicrously padded with a pillow Heather had picked up at Kohl's, and the snow-white synthetic beard was pulled up high to mask as many of my mean-looking features as possible, but the end result was more terrifying than merry. Away from Maureen, Heather's trembling, fawning demeanor had dissipated and was replaced by an exact duplicate of her boss' brand of abrasiveness. "That's Pete and Rebecca," Heather said sharply, introducing me to a pair of university drama students in green tights and gold metallic smocks. "They'll be your elves for tonight." I nodded graciously to the bored-looking sprites. "They keep the line moving and help out if you get a crier," Heather explained. Then she lectured me, "Don't spend a lot of time with each kid, but don't make it look like you're rushing them, either…the parents get really pissed off about that." I dismissed Heather with a wave of my gloved hand and addressed the elves directly with my own set of basic instructions. "None of the brats on my lap, no exceptions," I said without a trace of humor in my voice. "I expect the children to stand respectfully at the foot of my throne, and at the first sign of a temper tantrum or hysterical outburst, you are to lead them immediately back down the ramp and return them to their parents. No second chance, no three strikes." Heather attempted to regain control of the situation, but I cautioned my elves to be mindful that some of the children might very well be infested with head lice, and with that as my final word we made our way off to the mall's garish, glittering Winter Wonderland.

The first child tested and set in place Santa's ground rules. The tiny boy shrieked and screamed as if he had been jabbed with a hot poker, and although my elf Pete was close to six feet tall and burly, it took all of his gym-built strength to subdue the kicking, screeching little monster and then drag him down the curved sparkling red ramp with the candy cane railings back to a pair of horrified parents who wrestled with their young son like he was a badger caught in a trap until he exhausted himself and fell into a stupor. Silence settled over the yuletide scene for a moment as everyone from the elves and mothers and fathers to the children themselves digested the events that had just been served up cold. After I was certain that we had all come to a collective understanding of how to proceed in a manner that was dignified yet festive, I beckoned to the next child. A girl who was no more than six years old shuffle-ball-changed her way up the ramp, stopping before my throne to strike a rather unsettling pose with her hips cocked one way and her shoulders the other that made her look like a stunted Betty Grable. "I'm Ashley, I'm the best dancer in my class," the little girl announced. "No one likes a show-off, Ashley," I said, then I asked, "And what makes you think that you're the best dancer in your class?" "My mommy says so," Ashley proudly informed me. "Mommy says I'm better than Kristin, even if she gets the best solos." "Of course your mommy would say that," I told Ashley, "she has psychological problems." "What does that mean?" Ashley asked, sounding

155

more curious than concerned. "It means she's a very bitter, unhappy woman who forces you to take your dance classes even when you really want to stay home and watch TV or look up naughty things on your computer," I said. Ashley's tiny face appeared to suddenly age. "Don't worry," I said, attempting to reassure the girl, "someday Mommy will grow bored with you and focus her attention on the paper boy who just turned eighteen." "I still want to be the best dancer!" Ashley cut me off defensively. "But Kristin is the best dancer," I said, and the little girl reacted with a trembling lip and watery eyes. "Maybe something terrible will happened to Kristin, then you would be the best dancer!" I said in a genuine attempt to cheer up the tot. "That would be bad," Ashley murmured in a way that made me think she was fishing for encouragement. "Bad if you got caught," I whispered. "If you were very smart about it, no one would ever blame you, and that would be good." Ashley eyed me with an oddly mature expression, then nodded her head and joined the elf waiting to lead her away. I was about to give the signal for the next child to approach when I heard a loud scream, followed by a gasp that rose up from the crowd. My elf Rebecca was falling backward down the ramp, windmilling her arms wildly like Martin Balsam when he tumbled down Norman Bates' stairs in *Psycho*. Ashley began wailing, "Mommy, Mommy I didn't do it! It was an accident, it was an accident!"

"I'm Sean," the little boy told me. "Sean? What a pretty name…that's a girl's name," I said by way of a greeting. "No it's not!" "Yes it is." "Is not!" "Is too." We volleyed back and forth until I told him, "There's an actress named Sean Young. She went crazy and her career fizzled. That's probably why you never heard of her." Once again in charge, I asked, "So what would you like for Christmas, Sean?" "A bike and a G.I. Joe, one of the big ones," the boy said. "How about a bike and a G.I. Joe Rapid Strike Commando?" I offered, but Sean shook his head quickly back and forth and said, "I want a Navy SEAL." "So do I, Sean," I confided, "but sometimes we have to settle for what's available. If we were to get everything we wanted, then nothing would be special... and Sean, in the end nothing is special, not even a Navy SEAL." Sean looked down at his tiny boots, then turned and made his forlorn exit – away from Winter Wonderland, back to the dull ache of real life.

Ben was a blank, slack-jawed child with a paunchy face and a vacant look in his eyes who asked me to leave an archery set for him under the Christmas tree. "An archery set?!" I exclaimed with phony enthusiasm. "Why would you want that?" "So I can shoot birds and squirrels," the boy told me in a flat, lifeless voice. "Have you asked your parents to get you an archery set?" I inquired. The boy's face suddenly brightened as he said, "Oh, no! They're getting me a puppy!" I slipped my hand into the pocket of my red Santa jacket for the small notepad I carry with me to jot down insightful observations that spontaneously occur to me without deliberation or warning. Seven thousand years of roaming this old world has made me a pretty astute judge of character, and besides, I've watched enough *Criminal Minds* reruns that I can now spot a nascent serial killer with ease. I carefully composed my worries, jotted them down, pressed the folded slip of paper into Pete's hand, and discretely sent him off to deliver the troubling news to Ben's parents. The couple read the note together, each neatly printed word that starkly spelled out the unspeakable suspicions that they could never allow to break free from their most private tortured thoughts to become a fully formed concern. They looked up at me, looked at each other, then looked down at their phlegmatic boy. The husband put an arm around his wife's shoulder, and even from my lofty vantage point perched high above Winter Wonderland, I could see that they were worn down by a terrible worry no parent should ever bear. The sad little family turned and walked slowly away, disappearing into the sea of happy shoppers with their gaily-colored gift bags.

One by one they came, skipping, running, gamboling full of wonder and innocence up the glittery red ramp, and one by one they would leave a little older, a little wiser, a little slower, with shoulders slightly stooped and little brows furrowed, back to a world that suddenly seemed far less merry. "Do you love me, Santa?" Gretchen asked, holding her arms outstretched wide in a desperate gesture of all-encompassing affection. "No," was my simple, stripped-to-the-basics answer. "My mommy and daddy love me," Gretchen said optimistically, maintaining her extended reach. "You're confusing love with obligation," I said. "Mommy and daddy love you because they have no other choice; besides, they give you nice things and treat you like a princess to impress the neighbors and your mother's sisters, who are always looking for something to criticize." "But I love you!" Gretchen bleated with a hint of desperation in her squeaky, tinny voice, her pint-sized hands clenching into fists. "You only love me because you want Barbie shit and a Loopdedoo," I said, leaning in closer to the girl. "Do you love that smelly old man with the white beard sleeping next to the dumpster in the alley?" Gretchen dropped her hands to her sides and whispered with a hint of entitled anger, "I've been good, all year I've been good." I lounged back on my throne and crossed my legs. "Yeah, and so has that disfigured little boy on the bus sign who lives in one of those hot, dirty, horrible countries where people starve and die from drinking filthy water." Gretchen pouted. "What do you think he wants for Christmas—toys? Bullshit!" I said. "He wants a new god-damn face; he wants the flies to stop biting his sticky, misshapen lips...and what do you think he'll get? More pain, hunger, and despair...that's what he'll get." Gretchen backed away from my throne. "That's life, kid," I said, "the disappointment and heart-break and horror like a cloud of flies that torment you constantly, and all you can do is run as fast as those little legs will carry you to Christmas, then to Disney World, then to your birthday party, to one mirage after another – any goddamn thing that lets you to pretend the world is nice and pretty...and good." The little girl stood frozen in place. Pete looked up from checking Grindr messages on his iPhone and said, "Holy fuck!" I sent the wobbly child away with a cheerful, "Merry Christmas!" then rose and left the stunned crowd with a hearty, "And to all a good night!"

QUEEN OF THE OASIS LOUNGE

Given my general feelings of ill will toward the holidays, you probably assume that I spent New Year's Eve in gloating solitude contemplating the misery and disappointment sure to visit the world over the next twelve months, but in fact I welcomed in the new year at the Oasis Lounge. I wanted to avoid a New Year's Eve experience that required weeks of planning, a pricey cover charge, too-carefully-considered attire, and an unreasonable expectation of fun, so I chose for my destination the unassuming little storefront bar that I've passed by with barely a notice countless times. Aside from a few Mylar helium-filled balloons with curled foil streamers that could be bought at any supermarket in the days preceding a festive occasion, there was hardly a hint of New Year's Eve at the Oasis. It was nothing more than a typical Saturday night. Raised up high behind the bar were two long aquariums filled with murky water, blue gravel, and plastic plants. Several large, colorless fish hovered listlessly in the cloudy tanks. Maybe at one time long ago they were vibrantly colored and active creatures, but like everything at the Oasis, they had become faded, dull, and irrelevant. The moment

I pulled open the door I was hit by the stale beery atmosphere; a hint of stagnant old cigarette smoke still clung to the place years after smoking had become verboten, and The Flirts were singing on the jukebox: "PASSION...PASSION..." The next song up was Big Country's one and only hit with its signature bagpipe-sounding guitars, followed by The Human League. There were a few young, self-consciously sullen and disheveled hipster types, but the crowd was mostly made up of people much older. I didn't feel as if time had stood still in the dark, dingy confines of the Oasis, but rather that the world had turned its back on the place and its patrons. A smattering of cheers greeted the opening chords of John Mellencamp's "Jack and Diane," and several women danced. With eyes closed and heads tilted back, they raised their arms high in the air, squatted down, wiggled their butts, and then shimmied back up like she-cats in heat. It was a sad, clingy display that reached back to a day when they were much younger and the notion of Saturday night probably held a lot more promise.

I spied an empty bar stool, so I made my way through the crowd and sat down. "HI!" A small, slim woman named Mary with short, badly-dyed blonde hair and a Jimmy Buffet concert t-shirt worn over a long-sleeved jersey turned and shouted to me as if we were acquaintances reunited after a long absence of friendship. I returned her greeting and began to wish her a happy new year, which seemed appropriate, but she cut me off quickly and introduced me to her friends, Ed and Royce, seated on the stools next to her. During the course of my visit to the Oasis Lounge I learned a good deal about Mary and her two friends, none of the information being very personal or meaningful. Mary, Royce, and Ed were regulars at the Oasis – at least they were regulars on Wednesdays and Saturdays when the bar featured attractive drink specials right up to closing time. On

Mondays and Thursdays Mary, Ed, and a woman named Carol were regular customers at a dive called Mrs. O'Malley's Inn for the two-for-one Bloody Mary special, and on Sundays Mary, Royce, and another man who answered to "Cappy" took advantage of the free pizza and dollar beer night at Tommy's Tavern. Beyond drinking, I don't know what held these wretched souls together in friendship. They chattered and laughed non-stop as they told me one story after another about this night at that bar and that night at another bar until everything churned together into one drunken blur. All three were employed, but where and in what capacity I was never able to discover. Their jobs were brushed off as dead-ended drudgeries or low-man-on-the-totem-pole nuisances with phrases like, "I woke up just in time to make my shift," or "I'm taking off an extra day so I can have two short weeks." Their home lives were dismissed in similar fashion. Never once did Mary or her two companions show any interest in learning about me. They didn't inquire about who I might be or what brought me to the Oasis.

I've often been referred to as an egomaniac, and though I might understand why people would call me such, I've never been so vain or self-absorbed that I can't admit to failure. Looking back on my long existence, I've achieved some great and terrifying feats. It wasn't Helen who launched the thousand ships that ultimately destroyed Troy – it was me. Oh, not with beauty, but with the far more potent power of suggestion. I've set two world wars into motion by delivering the right words to the right people at the right time. Unleashing revolution and chaos on the world has been easy for me, but I ran into a brick wall trying to find out what heartbreak and mischance had brought Mary, Ed, and Royce to their pitiful states. I prodded and poked, asked the right questions without sounding too forward or prying. I masterfully led them to areas where the dark truth must surely lurk, and I slithered and wrapped myself around the tiny scraps of personal information they offered up, but all I accomplished was to inspire another volley of stories about the night Ed accidently hit Royce with a dart or when Mary broke the jukebox. Life is littered with the remains of tragedies and failures, and for every triumph someone in some way has to pay the price, but I came to the conclusion that Mary, Ed, and Royce had neither met any great collapse of fortune nor had ever experienced any crippling denouement. They were simply life's quiet little flops. I always look at the world in epic oversized terms, but in bleak dismal homes, on lonely street corners, and in dank neighborhood bars, one can find the sad, meaningless lives that clutch and grasp for a meager shred of purpose or place.

One by one, Mary then Ed then Royce would leave to stand on the street in front of the Oasis and smoke. The two remaining friends would guard the vacated barstool with the tenacity of a bull crocodile protecting his spot in the swamp. A man with a moustache and comb-over ordered a drink, then eyed Mary's empty stool with the obvious intentions of planting himself down for an extended stay. "That seat's taken!" Ed snapped brusquely as Royce protectively draped his coat over the barstool. I assumed Mary had stepped outside for a cigarette when I suddenly heard a clamor coming from the far corner of the room where the bar's single rest room was located. The bartender muttered, "Jesus Christ, not again!" and rushed to the ruckus while fumbling with his keys. He knocked on the rest room door and shouted, "Mary, I'm coming in! You all right?" Ed and Royce laughed and toasted each other. "First time this year!" Ed smiled and winked. The bartender made his way through the crowd with a blushing Mary trailing at his heels. Once again at his station behind the bar, he washed his hands and said, "Mary, I've told you over and over: make sure the seat's down before you sit."

She climbed back onto her bar stool and turned to Ed and Royce. "How many times have I done that?" she laughed. Mary smiled at me impishly and said, "I forgot to check if the damn seat was down, and I sat right in the toilet bowl…got stuck, and if wasn't for…" The other patrons began raising their drinks in Mary's direction as they laughed and cheered. She covered her face with her hands, shook her head vigorously from side to side, then hopped off of her bar stool, curtsied, and smiled a huge beaming smile. Everyone in the bar began chanting "Mary, Mary, Mary…"

I slipped out as Mary was taking her bows. The night's festivities were beginning to wind down, and people were leaving the clubs and parties and finding their way back into everyday life. I passed a group of young men who looked to be in their early thirties walking down the street, a hint of unsteadiness in their gait. "It's my project; I started it, I did all the work," one of them was saying to his friends, who frowned slightly out of concern, or maybe queasiness. Then he slurred, "I'm not letting those assholes take the credit when it was my…" as they trailed away through the slush and cold and dark that rang in a new year. A smartly-dressed couple around the same age as Mary and the gang in the Oasis stood on the curb waiting for a cab. The woman yawned and pulled the collar of her Maison Martin Margiela trench coat up around her chin as her husband flagged a taxi. "We should decide on the tile this week if we want the bathroom finished by spring," she said as a yellow painted Camry pulled to a stop at the curb. The group of young men passed the Oasis without notice; the middle-aged couple sailed away in their cab unaware that the dingy little bar was even there. I thought of the worn and bedraggled crowd in the Oasis – of Ed and Royce and of Mary basking in her moment with the Bo Deans' "Good Things" playing on the jukebox. Maybe she did find her sliver of purpose and place after all. She was the Queen of the Oasis Lounge…at least on Saturday and Wednesday nights.

WISDOM, PART II

SHINGLES

Alexios,

I'm upset and disappointed with my husband. We have had a long weekend planned to see the fall colors in Door County with another couple we are friends with. Our reservations have been made for a long while, and I was so looking forward to it. My husband Stan has just gotten shingles and is in quite a lot of pain and doesn't think he's in any condition to take the trip. Our friends Debra and Don are still going, of course, and I think it would be unfair for me to miss the trip, especially because my husband didn't get a shingles vaccination when I got mine at Walgreens. I told him when I got my shot that he should get one too, but like always, he never listens to me. I knew it was just a matter of time before this happened, but I didn't think it would crop up now and ruin my vacation. If I stay home with Stan, then all I'll hear about later is what a wonderful time Debra and Don had. I don't feel like I should be responsible for taking care of Stan because he could have avoided the problem if he had done what I told him to do. Should I go and enjoy my trip to Door County?

Carla

Carla,

Harry Truman went to his grave claiming that never once did he suffer a sleepless night over his decision to drop the bomb on Japan, but I can tell you he didn't doze off for even a moment between midnight and dawn when he sought my advice on the weighty matter. History will forever debate Harry's decision, but a verdict will never be reached. There was no right or wrong, good or bad, black or white choice for Truman to make – all he had before him were long months of caskets draped in blood red, white, and blue or an instant blinding hot nuclear finale. Life isn't simple, and even a gentle ripple on the water can announce the menacing presence of something big and sinister gliding just below the surface. Dive in and hope for the best. Every day presents you with a series of choices, but life rarely offers up anything pleasant on its pallet of options. More often than not you're asked to choose between walking across hot coals or a bed of nails, and Carla, I can tell you that whatever you decide to do, by the time your weekend trip limps to a conclusion, your feet will be either burned, or bloody. Winning isn't available; you're being forced to choose how you'd rather lose. Unfortunately, I can't offer a few soothing words that would send you off on your Door County getaway with a clear conscience and a peaceful soul, so the best I can do is to guide you through your not-so-agreeable situation.

Ever since you got pricked by the pharmacist at Walgreens, you've been hoping your husband would suffer the pain of shingles. You've been waiting to tell him that you were right, that he was stupid for ignoring your advice, and that he has no one to blame but himself for his misfortune. You got what you wished for, but every wish granted comes with a heavy price. Common decency should compel you to forgo the fall colors and gift boutiques so you can offer some comfort to your ailing spouse, but if you cancelled your vacation and stayed home with Stan, would you really be there to offer your husband assistance, or would you spend a miserable several days berating and blaming him for your own unfair mischance? And what of Stan? He might not feel abandoned if you traipsed off to Door County solo. I assume you've been married for quite some time, and by this point the pain of shingles is a small toll for Stan to pay for a few days free from your constant carping. Maybe he didn't get a shingles shot on your command because he's tired of taking orders from a woman who spends her every waking minute dictating his every single move. Enduring a dreadful weekend being hectored that maples trees have more pleasing colors than oaks for simply remarking, "Look at that one over there," probably doesn't rank very high on his list of favorite things, and I'll clue you in on a little secret: Stan doesn't want to follow you around quaint little shops browsing through curio cabinets of blown glass animal figurines and gift sets of assorted cheeses in rustic wooden crates tied with sisal. Your husband would much rather enjoy a relaxing weekend poolside in a warm and exotic location leering at nearly-naked trust fund babies on a cocaine- and booze-fueled bender. Cancelling your trip and staying home to minster to Stan wouldn't be pleasant, but it would put a feather in your cap of selflessness, and you could spend the next few years reminding him of your act of generosity every time he wanted to watch a football game on TV, but would you really gain a sense of satisfaction, or would it just place one more spot of rot on your decaying marriage?

So then, leave Stan and his shingles to languish at home and go to Door County with Debra and Don, but be warned; once you embark on the trip you will be no companion, fellow traveler, or equal, but instead you will find yourself occupying the unenviable position of interloper, parasite…fifth wheel. I remember as if it were only yesterday when the gentlest shift in the breeze turned a small fire in Nero's Rome into a colossus that consumed the imperial city. Just a whisper is enough to unleash a deadly avalanche, and a single misplaced word can cost the best-funded front runner a national election. The dynamic will shift the moment you tell Debra and Don of Stan's condition. You might not notice that they're holding hands in the front seat of the car as you sit in the back and point out the first blazing red tree along the way, but later you'll see them strolling arm in arm and realize that you're walking several steps behind, and you'll find that you're left on the sidelines as they exchange cute little jokes and endearments over hot apple cider and pumpkin muffins. A weekend with friends will have become a romantic couple's vacation that you've attached yourself to like a barnacle on the bottom of a party boat. At a wine tasting event, Debra and Don will nod to each other, smile, then buy a delicately fruity Sauvignon Blanc to save for their anniversary while you choose something cheap and bitter to drink alone in your room later that night. You'll deny the horrible reality of your predicament; you'll pretend that your imagination is playing a hideous trick on you, but when Debra and Don make dinner reservations for two at an intimate restaurant there will be no place left for you to hide from the mortifying truth. "But Carla, we all had a nice lunch together today," they'll explain with as much kindness as the uncomfortable situation can support. You'll subject Debra and Don to the icy silent treatment for the remainder of the weekend, and that will give you plenty of time to fill yourself with a burning resentment for Stan back home with his shingles, La-Z-Boy recliner, and TV show about those guys from Florida who catch alligators marauding in people's backyards and swimming pools.

Carla, when you make your choice and step forward, you will either plant your foot on burning coals or feel the sharp stab of nails. I don't know which is more painful, but I can tell you both will hurt. Stan's shingles will fade away, and Debra and Don will finish off their special bottle of wine, but your rancor will linger, taking its place with all of the other slights and grievances that you've accumulated and saved like souvenirs over the years to become one more curdled keepsake in your unhappy life.

Whatever you decide to do, have a great weekend!

THE BIG LIE

Alexios,

I've never written to anyone asking for advice before, but there's a first time for everything, I guess. I have a problem that is my own fault, and I don't want to bring it up to any of my friends, so I had nowhere to go to for help. I'm 33 years old and have been married to a great woman for 5 years. We dated in high school, then broke up. We met up a few years later and got back together and then got married. Everything is great, but I cheated. It wasn't an affair or anything like that, just a one-time thing. I thought I could just forget about it, but I caught an STD...not the bad one, a curable one, thank God. Now my wife will definitely find out. What can I do so my marriage doesn't get wrecked?

Ben

Ben,

First of all, congratulations on contracting one of the better STDs. I can tell you how to save your marriage, but you need to come to terms with the fact that it will never be the same again, and that your relationship will go through some difficult and lasting changes no matter what course of action you take. You can be honest with your wife, tell her everything that happened and beg her forgiveness, but be warned: with forgiveness comes penance, and you'll be tortured with a lifetime of atonement. Life is a constant, relentless struggle to gain the best position. That's why people change lanes on the highway, marry up, and discard friends who have lost their usefulness. There are no equal partnerships; not everyone is on the same footing, and there is no 50/50. Only one person calls the plays, and someone always has to occupy the back row in the team photo. Of course, the dynamics are constantly shifting, so today's star can be tomorrow's utility player, but once you've accepted defeat – once you've exposed your throat – you've eliminated yourself from the game completely. An admission of guilt to your wife would guarantee you a spot on the bench…until-death-do-you-part.

You're a liar. I'm not pointing an accusatory finger at you or holding you up to be singled out. Everyone is a liar. When was the last time you said, "It was nice to see you again" with any honesty…and when was the last time you said, "I love you," and meant it? You lie to cover your ass at work, you lie to keep your friends at a comfortable distance, and you lie to avoid tedious family obligations. When asked your opinion on any manner of topic, you respond with dishonesty in hopes that you'll appear cooler or smarter than you really are. People lie to mask the truth—oh, not a small, mildly uncomfortable truth, but the fundamental, unbearable truth of their lives. Life is a performance art piece of deception, it's the only way people can survive the ordeal. "Does this outfit make me look fat?" "Is she out of my league?" "Have you been faithful to me?" "Doctor, what are my chances?" You certainly don't want an honest answer – you want a lie…a lie that you can dig your fingers in deeply, grab onto as tightly as you can, and believe with all your heart.

Ever since man climbed down from the trees and formed tribes, power has been the most precious of treasures, and perfidy even more than blunt force has always been the key to seizing and possessing control. I'm not sure when I came up with the idea, but it was a very long time ago, thousands and thousands of years ago, that I began to mold the thoughts of the most ambitious of men – men who lustfully eyed thrones and crowns and the highest of religious stations, and I advised them to lie. I told them to recreate themselves with stories of glorious lineage leading back through the fog of time and memory to fabled heroes whose dubious reality had become shrouded in a sparkling haze of myth. Eventually I told them to claim a bloodline that snaked and crawled all the way to the gods themselves, and it worked. The unruly masses were thrilled to believe. The lie was more intoxicating than the truth could ever be, and so the pharaoh was transformed into the gods' king on earth, emperors proclaimed their own divinity, and the pope became infallible. But in these modern times when royalty is frowned upon, power can be gained by claiming not an exalted history, but by embracing an exaggeratedly humble past. Everyone is an everyman despite a luxurious compound in Hyannis Port or a Swiss bank account or a successful family construction business. Lincoln was elected president with help from the homespun stories told of his raggedy early years, and Richard Nixon campaigned on Pat's cloth coat. Millionaire George W. Bush was a regular guy, and movie star Ronald Reagan acted like your best friend. Barack Obama presented a pedigree as a lowly community organizer with a burden of student loan debt. Before long, the day will come when no one can ever hope to plant their keister in the leather chair behind the desk in the Oval Office unless they conjure up a past that includes grandparents who ate out of garbage cans and a childhood spent with a single mom in a refrigerator carton next to a dumpster. On the campaign trail and at political conventions, the Ivy League years and trust funds are all but ignored in favor of shameless pandering to the lower bracket. Lie to me; I don't care how ridiculous or insulting, tell me anything but the horrible truth. "A burning bush?" Power hungry Moses stared at me in wary disbelief, but I assured him, "Trust me, they'll believe you." He trusted me, and they believed.

"If you tell a lie big enough and keep repeating it, people will eventually come to believe it. The lie can be maintained only for such time as the State can shield the people from the political, economic, and/or military consequences of the lie. It thus becomes vitally important for the State to use all of its powers to repress dissent, for the truth is the mortal enemy of the lie, and thus by extension, the truth is the greatest enemy of the State." Joseph Goebbels.

Ironically, I gave those words of wisdom to both Dr. Goebbels and Winston Churchill. The prime minister digested them, processed them, and used my guidance to create an enduringly heroic myth around himself and his nation, but Goebbels found a more terrifying meaning in my council, then shamelessly repeated it word-for-word as his own deadly observation. Joseph Goebbels wasn't very bright, but while he lacked sanity and a razor-sharp intellect, he did possess a stunning understanding of dishonesty. Germany's propaganda minister knew the difference between the big lie and the average fib. The big lie is sweeping and conceptual; it can't be easily fact-checked or disputed, and it's not bogged down by the inconvenient weight of specific incidents. It cuts to the emotional bone and sinks its roots in the marrow and blossoms with poisonous flowers in the soul. I'm afraid the golden age of dishonesty is over. No one tells the big lie anymore. I blame Bill Clinton. He turned the art of lying into cheap burlesque the moment he wagged his finger and said, "I did not have sex with that woman, Monica Lewsinski." Mendacity has never been the same after that shoddy performance. Clearly he wasn't telling the truth, and he made no effort to suspend disbelief. The lie was simply a dare, a poke in the eye, a brazen "Oh yeah? What are you going to do about it?" It set a very low standard for fabrications to come.

I've lost count of the number of times I've advised others to lie, but my advice has always been honestly given. I encourage people's dishonesty, but I rarely lie myself. For me, telling the truth is much more interesting…and unforgiving. A few years ago I met a man in my neighborhood who was dying of cancer. Every time I encountered Joe on the street, he would excitedly inform me of a new treatment he was investigating or of a clinic somewhere he was certain could stop the disease that rushed through his body like Sherman marching to the sea. His family offered the type of optimism that always revolved around a wedding or graduation that loomed on the near horizon – a marker or milestone barely within reach. "I'm gonna beat this damn thing–I know that," Joe would tell me through the pain as he quickly grew more shriveled and weak. I would listen and nod my head, but I always remained silent. One evening Joe saw me in a coffee shop and stopped in. He winced as he took a seat at my table, caught his breath, and told me of a new organic diet he had begun to try. "If I give it time I think it might actually—" he began to say, but I interrupted, "Joe, you're like one of those Japanese pilots holed up on a tiny island in the Pacific still fighting the war years after Hirohito surrendered." There was silence, then he told me about a movie he planned to see the next day. I never saw Joe again. He probably avoided me, but several weeks later I was reading the obituaries and saw his name.

Ben, I suggest you lie. Say nothing until the missus shows symptoms of the malady herself, then blame her for the venereal affliction haunting your home. Make no mistake: I'm not talking about a little white lie or a fib, but instead, you would need to lie on a truly epic scale. The content of the lie isn't important, but the quality of the deception is vital. Dishonesty is a work of art, and like a masterful painting, your lie must draw a person in, captivate or terrify them, dazzle or humble them. Your tongue is the brush, your words are the paint, and the truth is your canvas. Adorn the canvas with your creation, recreate the truth...blame your wife. Shed real tears, show true anger, offer heartbroken forgiveness, but never waver, never lose focus, and never falter in your embrace of the deception. Before you can convince anyone else, you must convince yourself...you must believe your own lie. Let the lie seep in and saturate you until it becomes part of your DNA. Fact and fiction blur when you live the lie with total conviction. Don't expect your wife to "believe" you, but if you breathe in your own dishonesty, sustain yourself with your own lie, well, she will begin to have doubts, and that's all you need: doubt. Your wife will wonder if maybe she sat on the wrong toilet seat in the ladies' room of the restaurant when she joined her co-workers for a birthday lunch; she'll regret trying on that bathing suit at a discount department store. The lie will become a part of your marriage. Your wife will never fully trust you, and the passion of your lie will possess you, so you'll begin to eye her with suspicion as well...but you will survive to battle on.

Lie to your wife, Ben, save your marriage or salvage what's left of it. Lie with your soul, lie so profoundly it will rock the heavens. Honor the tradition of deceit. Lift the art of lying from its pitiful morass. Make me proud. Dishonesty is a private triumph, though, so don't ever expect to be celebrated or lauded for an expertly executed chicanery. Your lie will be a precious secret hidden in your heart. There will be no "Job well done," no hearty slap on the back, but your lie will take on a life of its own, it will stop you dead in your tracks and send you off in a new direction. Be strong, be resolute, and you'll do just fine.

Good luck, Ben.

"...for the truth is the mortal enemy of the lie."

POISE

Alexios,

Several years ago my wife of 43 years, Marie, passed away. We had a wonderful life together, we were the perfect pair. Marie was the center of my life, and I was devastated when she died. I couldn't imagine living without her, but I've recently reached the point where I'm ready to date again. I've gone out with a number of women now...most of them were very nice...but I haven't felt any of them were "the one" until I met Cheryl. We met on an online dating site for mature singles, and from our first meeting I knew there was a strong connection. We have gone out on a handful of dates, and we enjoy the same things, and I feel there is already a bond forming. She may be the one I've been hoping to meet. Last night we went to see a romantic comedy, and after the movie Cheryl invited me to her home for dessert and coffee. I excused myself to use her bathroom, and after I washed my hands I opened the doors of the cabinet under the sink and saw a box of Poise incontinence pads. We are going out again this week, but I've found myself going back onto the dating site and looking through more profiles. I feel guilty, I feel like I'm being unsympathetic about her little problem and selfish that I'd like to find a perfect partner, but I'm hoping to find "the one," and now I'm not sure it's Cheryl.

Bruce

My one and only, my one true love, the one...

Bruce, when you stroll through the stately old section of the cemetery with the cooling shade of age-old oak trees and solemn monuments carved into shapes like huge crosses or life-size angels to the sun-bleached expanse of lawn with neat rows of small, flat headstones pounded down even with the turf so the grounds keepers can glide over the loved ones on their tractor mowers in a single continuous pass...whose grave are you dropping a pot of geraniums onto? Wasn't Marie "the one"? How many one true loves does one person deserve, or rightly expect to have?

One: being or amounting to a single unit or individual or entire thing, item, or object rather than two or more; a single: one woman; one nation; one piece of cake.

Everyone yearns to discover the magical, mystical, mysterious, mathematically indivisible "one." Jennifer Aniston famously found her "one and only," then Angelina Jolie found the same one. When your one true love cheats on you or steals from the bank account to buy escort services or drugs, can you simply subtract one from one and go back to the beginning for a fresh start, or have you used up your "one" on a bad one? Wasn't Marie your "one," and is it fair to all the lonely hearts of the world that you are now looking for another one? Some people never find "the one," and you expect two? Bruce, after more than four decades of being half of a whole, aren't you ready to be the one in your own right? You and Cheryl don't really enjoy the same things. You didn't enjoy enduring that saccharine romantic change-of-life comedy with aging A-list stars; you would have preferred to see a movie with explosions and gunfire. When you went to Cheryl's house after the film, you didn't want flourless chocolate cake and hazelnut coffee; you wanted to get laid.

I'm often asked if I ever found my one true love at some point during my long existence, and I always answer honestly, "Yes." Seven thousand years ago I found my one true love, my one and only, the one…I found myself. I've never understood the appeal in dragging someone around like a conjoined twin and having every move, every decision turned into a discussion, a negotiation, a compromise, a battle of wills that ends with one winner and one loser. Don't waste your time calling me selfish; I happily admit to the fact. I'm not interested in how your day went, I don't care to hear what you ordered from a catalogue, and I don't want to spend an evening salving your insecurities or explaining my whereabouts. The marriage vow says "for better or for worse, for richer, for poorer, in sickness and in health," but who really needs a pledge to stick around for "better," "richer," and stellar "health"? The very idea of a "one true love" or "soul mate" is a prison that locks you into cell alongside "worse," "poorer," and "sickness." Once the bloom is off the rose and you're left with a dried stem and thorns, a moral guilt-trip of those prickly nettles binds you to a situation that you should have politely excused yourself from years before.

Bruce, if a nineteen-year-old Victoria's Secret model had invited you to her home for coffee and dessert, I doubt that you would have been concerned in the least by the discovery of Poise incontinence panty liners in her bathroom cabinet, but the presence of that purple box under the sink of a less-than-youthful Cheryl made you feel old. The other night I was watching a cable news show that devoted much of its time to the various national legislators who had been caught red-handed with an array of prostitutes, rent-boys, and congressional pages. Without fail, each commercial break presented an advertisement for

Cialis that featured a variety of semi-fit-looking older gentlemen becoming pharmaceutically aroused by ogling their older wives who were engaging in some type of antic devised to make them appear madcap or girlish. Those commercials aren't about golden-years-coupling or revived hard-ons; they're about reclaiming something lost – about reaching back past hundreds of mortgage payments, the crushing weight of a career you were never very interested in, and self-absorbed offspring who bled you dry then grew up and moved out, to a time when finding "the one" seemed easier than finding yourself. The AARP-aged congressmen and senators with their stooped shoulders, creaky voices, and young bedmates could never sell Cialis. They don't look like the Brawny Paper Towel man's father walking barefoot on the beach while his wife skips and hops like she's never let go of high school. It's not about now, it's all about then. Bruce, if you answered another profile on the mature singles website, walked into Starbucks for your first date, and found Marie, she wouldn't be "the one" from forty years ago; she'd just be an old lady. You want to snip away the decades of disappointment and failures, weariness and boredom, "what ifs" and "why nots" and connect your youth and its notion of a boundless future with the end run you find yourself now facing. You're sprinting to the finish line alone; everyone does in his own way. I drift through the ages, solitary, unencumbered, free, but you've spent the best years of your life shackled to a ponderous concept of incomplete self. Why do you want to wrap things up by forcing yourself into a cookie-cutter form shaped by a lifetime of someone else's problems? What you need to find are fishing buddies, or a golf partner and a paid companion for a night once a month, not "the one." You've had that all along…just look in the damn mirror.

IT COULDN'T HAVE HAPPENED
TO A NICER GUY

Alexios,

I have been married for two years. A few weeks ago my wife gave birth to our son...our first child. We weren't trying, but we were very excited when Meghan found out she was expecting. I was in the delivery room, and it was a totally awesome experience until the nurse brought us the baby. Even all shriveled up and stuff, I could tell he looked just like my brother, not like me at all. Everybody in the family has seen the baby, but no one has mentioned anything about it yet. The baby looks more and more like my brother Ethan every day. Should I say something about it, or just shut up? I've given Meghan everything she's wanted, and I've always been there for Ethan. I'm a nice guy. I can't believe something like this could happen.

Connor

Connor,

Millions of hearts were warmed by a striking photograph of a lion cub meeting his father for the first time. The huge male lion, set majestically in profile against a cloudless blue sky, regarded his tiny offspring nose-to-nose in an image that inspired a multitude of comments from the farthest reaches of the World Wide Web that were sweeter than the most saccharine sentiment Hallmark has ever manufactured. Generously sprinkled in amongst the reactions expressed in cuddly baby-talk were melancholy reflections on the cold, callous state of humanity as compared to the gentle purity of nature, but the moment captured for all time (or at least the foreseeable future) in that remarkable photo was savage in its purity, not gentle. At six to eight weeks of age, lion cubs leave their hidden dens, and the leader of the pride will sniff them to confirm his own scent. If the stink of a different paternity is detected, Mufasa will immediately kill and devour Simba on the spot. The circle of life is drawn with a switchblade-sharp line. A pair of guppies greedily gulps down their own fry, not with evil intent, but rather, compelled by the timeless urge to feed. Mother alligators violently guard their nests, but once the hatched babies have become links in the food chain, Mama will casually consume the little ones. During the hardships of famine and drought, animals routinely destroy their own young, and even in the best of times, the strongest of the brood are fed while the weakling is starved, and the slightest imperfection is enough to send a baby hurtling from the nest or burrow. When man presumed to distance himself from his animal cousins, he disengaged from the primitive impulses dictated by nature and soon began to see things through a prism of politics and poetry. Existence became symbolic, and life itself was transformed into a mystical journey with well-defined rules of the metaphysical road, but even from an intellectually elevated state, people have routinely disposed of their young, whether to satiate the blood lust of a demanding god or to balm a burning torment in their own mind.

Many years ago, when work on the Great Sphinx of Giza had

only just begun, a wealthy and well-connected physician invited me to take an evening sail down the Nile on his splendidly appointed boat. He was a man of scrupulous standards, and even though I expended considerable effort, I was unable to dislodge any useful private information about his titled and powerful patients. All of the guests present on the sumptuous vessel were captivated by the host's charm and decorum. The doctor and his wife had recently become parents for the seventh time, but they had made the unexpected decision to reject the child and had left the infant exposed to perish in the roasting sun of the desert. The birth wasn't clouded by the scandal of uncertain lineage, nor did the baby exhibit any signs of infirmity or physical deformity. The physician, a slender man with precise features and an elegant manner, casually waved away a cloud of ravenous mosquitoes that had risen up from the dank river and said with matter-of-fact aloofness, "We just didn't like the looks of the damned thing." The physician's haughty, persnickety air of well-mannered indifference was just a curtain covering the true beastliness of human nature.

Connor, when the delivery room nurse presented Ethan's bastard for your inspection, the ancient instincts of nature kicked in, and you immediately realized the baby wasn't yours – that the parking valet had handed you the keys to another man's jalopy. A polite, civilized society forbade you from eating the infant, but in the darkest, most primal recesses of your being, you probably gave it a fleeting consideration before struggling to conceive of a more socially acceptable manner to unburden yourself of the dreadful lifelong responsibility for your brother's flushed, wrinkled, toothless spawn. You're definitely in a pickle, and allow me to update that old 16th century slang to its less whimsical but more blunt modern equivalent: Connor, you're fucked, and it couldn't have happened to a nicer guy.

"I'm a nice guy. I can't believe something like this could happen."

Perhaps if you hadn't spent so much time bowing to your wife's every whim and propping up your brother each time he stumbled, you might have been somewhat less nice but a bit more perceptive and a tad wiser. How far do you think "nice" gets you—to the Oval Office, or the papal throne? Presidents, prime ministers, and dictators don't become world leaders because they're nice. They body-slam the competition and humiliate their rivals with ease. Did Madonna rise to international superstardom because she's a swell person? How about Augustus, Stalin, or Steven Spielberg? I haven't survived for 7,000 years because I'm a darn nice fella. Connor, I'm not suggesting you abandon the baby in the scorching desert heat, but I am telling you to dump the brat in your brother's lap and wash your hands of the sordid story. Climb into the Enola Gay, drop Little Boy, and shine the light of motherfucking truth on this sorry situation. The light of truth isn't easy on the eyes, and it doesn't cast a soft warm glow that makes you look ten years younger in your bedroom. It's a searing flash that leaves a scorched landscape of smoldering cinders in its wake. People prefer a gauzy, harmless fiction over cold, hard fact – a fantasyland where everything is lined up perfectly, nothing is out of place, and goodness is richly rewarded. Don't bet on it. You can't make the team, get the corner office, or lock down the deal without throwing a few hard elbows and landing some punches. No matter how sleek and sophisticated, advanced, enhanced, digitized, and progressive life has become, this is still the same vicious world it's been from the start. The first monster that crawled out of the primordial slime eons ago realized that to inherit the earth, sometimes you have to eat your own.

But don't let me stop you, be the good guy…say nothing,

hold it all inside for an agonizing private passion play performed over a lifetime in three unbearable acts of anger, resentment, and regret. Turn a deaf ear, if you can, to the snide remarks and smirking innuendos whispered at every family get-together by the more crass members of your clan. Force yourself to smile with fake pride at each milestone that records your happy little family's history as you mark off the inches grown year after bitter year with the nub of a pencil on the doorframe that leads into the kitchen. Jump up and cheer at soccer games and pat your wife's arm as Ethan's son graduates with honors from high school. He'll pick your pocket for a college education, then hold his hand out expecting more when he gets married, and there will be nothing you can do but dutifully act the role of "Dad." Other children will certainly follow, not because you really want them, but because you need them to establish credibility, at least in your own troubled mind. Don't trust Meghan or try to convince yourself that this heartbreak is an outlier…every pattern has a starting point, and the past always haunts the future. The next child to come along could very well bear a suspicious resemblance to your best friend, and the subsequent little tyke might look disturbingly like your father. The only place for you to go is down, deeper and deeper into yourself to a depth where you can't feel a goddamn thing until you drown in a black ocean of denial and best intentions. When it all comes to an end, your brother's son might deliver your eulogy…think about that, then try to rest in peace.

That's all I can offer you, Connor. Good luck…and congratulations, I guess.

SNAPSHOTS

AS GOOD AS IT GETS: GREG

His name was Greg, and simply by accident or by chance, he became my friend for a brief shared moment. The first thing I noticed was his smile, big and bright, and by all appearances Greg seemed to be a very happy fellow.

A band I enjoy performed at a recent street festival, and fortunately, they were scheduled to play in the evening, so I was able to attend the show. I worked my way steadily past the vendors selling funnel cakes, tropical drinks in hollowed-out pineapples, handmade jewelry, and cheap sunglasses as I sifted through the crowd until I had situated myself only a short distance from the stage. Midway into the first song a voice close to my ear loudly informed me that the band was "awesome." I acknowledged the remark with a quick nod before returning my attention to the stage, but by the time the musicians finished their second selection I had learned that the voice belonged to Greg, and that he was pleased to make my acquaintance. Lifting his baseball cap and waving it in several directions at the same time, Greg told me that he had become separated from his group of buddies. "They're over there I guess...I don't know," he said, and so in the absence of his companions I became his friend. The concert was nothing more than a soundtrack – a backdrop to Greg's life story told to me in jumbled, vaguely drunken and disjointed scraps of personal information. Nothing he shared was compelling or even interesting in the least...not the story of his recent break-up with an unfaithful girlfriend, not the planned weekend trip to Las Vegas with his brother, not his gym routine or the problems he had with his car. But he possessed an openness, an earnestness that made me wonder how he could smile so easily when his life was so dull. Greg is employed by a large corporation known for its processed cheese products, boxed meals, and frozen pizzas. I can't describe to you his exact function with the company, but his job by all indications involves maintaining computer systems that allow the marketing people to track and assess the popularity of their sodium- and fat-larded products. Work wasn't a topic that Greg showed much enthusiasm for, and he quickly told me that he was taking the following Monday as a vacation day so he could "get trashed all weekend." The band began their signature song, inspiring Greg to unleash a loud "Whooo!" and raise his sticky cup of stale, flat beer over his head. As the tune concluded, Greg nodded, smiled, and quietly spoke a few of the lyrics. He looked at me, repeated the words, and said, "Incredible, awesome...I...you know...I write poetry...well...sometimes I do...a few poems...I've..." Suddenly much more interested in this stranger, I turned like a crocodile sensing the movement of an animal at the river's edge, like a shark picking up the vibrations of a seal in distress. "Oh!" Greg quickly added, "I don't... you know, read them anywhere, or you know...I've never shown them to any...I just..." At that moment, fate reached down with a hand of kindness and touched Greg's shoulder. "Hey, asshole!" one of his friends shouted through the crowd. Greg slapped me on the back and said, "I better get back to my buds, bro." As I worked my way out of the churning throng of people, I saw Greg huddled closely together with his small group of friends. He smiled broadly at a raised cell phone that would capture an image to be posted and shared and tagged and liked on Facebook. I suspect Greg's friends knew nothing about the crushing boredom of his job, the little disappointments that add up one day after another, or of the poems he wrote in his solitude. I suspect they didn't see the sadness behind his smile.

Perhaps my unique insight into life or my thousands of years of experience led me to take a seat in front of my computer, turn on the camera, and speak words of comfort to emotionally embattled young people all over the world. Certainly enough entertainers and athletes, politicians and gadflies, from Barack Obama to members of the Chicago Cubs to Stephen Colbert and Hillary Clinton, had offered up tales of their own horrid high school days or inspiring words of encouragement ending with the declaration, "It gets better," so why shouldn't my voice be added to the eclectic mix as well? I cleared my throat, collected my thoughts, and wondered if it might be best to call upon my ancient perspective and give an historical context to the weighty subject matter I meant to address. I could mention how catty and cruel the Egyptians had been or maybe describe how the ancient Persians were homophobic bullies until Alexander the Great came along and showed them who was boss or explain how The Terror in France faded away in time along with La Revolution. *Things eventually change*, I would tell the bullied and beleaguered youth, but in all honesty I could never say, "It gets better." I stared for a moment at my pale, ghostly face on the computer screen and then spoke from my heart. "I wish I could pat you on the arm and tell you that it gets better, but 'it' simply 'is.' 'It' is cancer and penury and an unfaithful lover; 'it' is boredom, failure, and disappointment. 'It' is the constant battle to find a seat at the table, to get a word in edgewise, to hold on for dear life. 'Better' is only a temporary rest from 'worse' – a brief, dread-filled cease-fire until the carnage begins anew. The fat kid who bullies you on the playground probably goes home to a drunken father who beats the hell out of him; the mean girls who mock you know in the darkest, clammiest recess of their hearts that their best years are being squandered in the wasteland of high school. 'Better' resides like a mirage just beyond everyone's clutching reach. Make no mistake: the world isn't mean-spirited or deliberately cruel. Life is not concerned with you, it doesn't even notice you...it's simply savagely indifferent in the most unfeeling, brutally primitive fashion. Survival, plain and simple – people are no different than hyenas snarling and snapping and fighting over the same scrap of torn, rotten flesh. Life grinds blindly along on its relentless path of least resistance, crushing anything and anyone too frightened, too tired, or too defeated to get out of its way..." I sat back and thought about my words, thought about the horrors I've unleashed over the ages and of the horrors that have found their own way into the world without my assistance. I doubt anyone believes that it will get better, but most people cling to a hope that it won't get worse. I submitted my video to the website that promises better things to come, but it was never posted. The blunt, honest words I spoke never took their place alongside those of the celebrities and commoners all offering that empty promise, "It gets better."

I made my way out of the street festival past groups of people eating sloppy Mexican or Thai food from flimsy red and white checkered cardboard dishes. They bellowed and brayed to be heard above the din of the crowd and the music blaring from the bands playing bad covers, digital dance tunes, or indie rock. The stench of greasy bratwurst and Italian sausage mingled with body odor, cigarette smoke, and a hint of vomit. A group of guys in baggy shorts and sweaty t-shirts pointed and gave a thumbs-up to several girls with smeared make-up and rumpled sundresses who were waiting in a long line leading up to a row of lopsided aqua-blue plastic porta-potties. "Stay together, everybody!" a mother called out as her family, holding hands, pushed their way through the throng like ducks trying to cross an expressway. Greg was standing in a sizable knot of people at a kiosk selling beer. Waiting patiently for his turn, he looked hot and tired, and no smile masked his inner sadness. His face was simply blank. Reaching up, he ran a hand over his stubbled jaw and nodded his head slightly...lost in his private poetry. Greg's life has probably never been difficult. I highly doubt he knows what it's like to have been tortured by bullies or lacerated by hateful words and threats or that he was ever cast aside by family or shunned by neighbors. Greg lives in a small apartment that's nice enough and kept reasonably clean. He's well-liked at work and can afford some simple pleasures. No one ever had to reassure Greg that "it gets better," but behind the smile he offered the vendor as he took the red plastic cup spilling over with beer, Greg worried that this might be as good as it gets. That's life, Greg. That's it, my friend.

WAITING FOR THE BUS TO NOWHERE: HARRIET

Night and day, darkness and light.

Honesty hides from the glaring light of day in the comforting shadows of night, and truth moves freely through the dark. Many regard my existence as a curse, a cross to bear, a Jacob Marley chain of misery binding me to an endless midnight, but I've never viewed it in that way. The night is my home. Life, exhausted from the courtesies and pretenses constructed as shields from the day's unforgiving, prying brightness, drags itself weary, unguarded, and naked into the sheltering dark…and each night I am there, waiting and watching as life exposes itself as the pallid, sickening creature it truly is. Admittedly, I do face some annoyances and limitations. Sometimes when I watch a movie or view a photographic spread in a magazine, I wonder what it would be like to experience all of those dazzling colors that only ignite under the rays of the sun. Less lyrically and more practically, useful businesses aren't always open and available when I'd like them to be…even public transportation withholds a good portion of its convenience once the sun has set.

I prepared myself for a long wait. There was no trace of a bus as far down the street as I could see. "Well, you're standing here, and I'm standing here, so we might as well talk," a voice tinged with the remnants of a drawl suddenly made me realize that I wasn't alone in the bus shelter, although when I looked from side to side I could find no companion…until I lowered my glance and discovered a very short old woman standing next to me, as wide as she was tall, with bushy white hair that I could tell had once been red. Not in the mood to make a new friend, I smiled and turned away—or up, I should say, but Harriet was determined, and reluctantly I found myself making her company. Immediately upon completing our introductions, Harriet asked me to guess her age. I have a sharp eye for such things, but I added a handful of years to my estimate in hopes that she would take offense sufficient enough to end our fledgling friendship. After a moment of surprise followed by another of annoyance, the old woman collected herself and said with a crinkled smile, "I'll bet you don't know how many grandchildren I have." Harriet happily shook her head in a strangely childlike fashion when I offered incorrect guesses on the number of grandchildren, regular, great, and great-great, that she could claim as her own. "Conversation" would never correctly describe what I shared with Harriet in the bus shelter. The old woman showed no interest in learning anything about me or my life, which was just as well, and our exchange languished as a one-sided affair with my contribution limited to those times when I was required to guess my way to some bit of information about her moth-eaten life. In the course of her eighty-eight years, Harriet had buried two grandchildren, a couple more of the great-great variety, and, most recently, one of her daughters. She had the type of remarkably round, rubbery pale pink face that looked as if it were made of Silly Putty, and her expression, from happy to sad, could change in the blink (or in Harriet's case, the wink) of an eye, but it always returned to what I can only call a self-satisfied grin. Her lifetime spanned remarkable events: a great depression, a polio epidemic, a world war, a cold war, a man on the moon, the Beatles, and America's first black president, but Harriet seemed oblivious to it all. She was the center of her own drab universe where everything revolved around her like bleak icy moons. "I've been married seventy-five years…seventy-five!" Harriet told me, tapping my arm for emphasis. "Have you ever known anyone married that long?" Before I could answer, she smiled slyly and said, "Every morning Dad and I still take our shower together…he even washes my behind! What do you think about that?!" Harriet held my arm tightly to keep me from backing away and gushed, "A lot of people are married fifty years, but seventy-five…that's the diamond anniversary!" Once I dismissed the image of Harriet receiving a thorough scrubbing in the shower, I realized something wasn't quite right about the old lady's story. "How old were you when you got married?" I asked in a voice innocent enough to raise no suspicion. "Sixteen," Harriet said with a proud smile. "I was a young one." I paused, then said, "But if you're eighty-eight years old that would mean…" Harriet released my arm and stared at me blankly, then stammered, "Oh…I don't know what difference it makes….it's…seventy-two…seventy-two, I've been married seventy-two years. Dad…he's not doing so well…he can still get around, but he's…I don't think he has much longer." In all likelihood, Harriet won't reach her milestone. The old woman rooted through her purse – a large tote-style bag made of unconvincing fake leather that was cracked and peeling around the seams. She sorted through a jumbled mass of receipts, paper prayer pamphlets, and coupons until she retrieved a handful of snapshots from a pocket with a broken vinyl zipper. Harriet fanned the photographs out like a deck of cards. "That's Gary," she said as she leafed past a picture of a sullen young man with a greasy mullet and bags under his blank eyes. "He's one of my great-grand-sons...he was arrested last week," she said, shaking her head. "I don't know why...this time. I guess it doesn't matter anymore." Harriet held up a creased photograph of an obese woman with a cigarette and missing tooth. "My granddaughter Ellen. She's get-ting married this spring...her third time, I think." The old lady's face brightened. "Here's Dad," she beamed, handing me the pic-ture. Harriet was a sixteen-year-old bride, and Dad was nineteen in the faded sepia-toned image that was captured long before life had sent Harriet racing desperately for a milestone that would signal the arrival of the end run.

Thousands of years before Harriet exchanged vows with her husband, I reclined on a silk upholstered couch in the magnifi-cent villa of a Roman nobleman living in Damascus as a high-so-ciety wedding celebration commenced. "She looks rather...com-mon," I whispered to the woman occupying the couch next to mine and nodded to the bride situated beside her well-connect-ed groom. "Common?!" Sestis laughed. "The Scipiones should be ashamed choosing a girl like that, but her family is worth a fortune," she shrugged. "Really? They seem so vulgar," I said, causing Sestis to sit up and slide in closer to me. "Oh, they are!" she excitedly hissed. "Imports from the east...that's where they made their money, but to be honest, they're really nothing more than peddlers who made it big...and the Scipiones are strapped for cash, they're broke...so...well, here we are. A match made by the gods themselves," she laughed. As the evening unfolded, Ses-tis pointed out various guests and family members, and she told me their tales through the most salacious gossip. The groom had fathered a multitude of bastards with the household slaves, a cer-tain dowager was nearly destitute after paying off her children's gambling debts, and a well-regarded senator who showed the ef-fects of an over-abundance of wine was said to mercilessly beat both his wife and his mistress whenever he got drunk. The gilded and bejeweled room was filled with the exceptionally wealthy and privileged, but they all behaved like the seedy side of your family or like the trashy neighbors down the street who live in the dilapidated house with the unkempt lawn. Celebrities and socialites who exhibit stunningly poor taste, bad judgment, and crude behavior are rabidly embraced by the public. Everything, no matter how unseemly, glitters with fascination in the glow of wealth. But although adorned with ostentatious riches, the privileged are as coarse and vulgar as the unwashed masses, and without their fortunes they would captivate no more attention than Harriet's brood. Money makes them interesting and important. Money makes them matter. *60 Minutes, Entertainment Tonight, People Magazine*, and *TMZ* have no interest in Harriet's bargain basement story. Lacking the proper bank account and investment portfolio, her life is just a low-rent sideshow far off the midway.

I sat down beside Harriet on the narrow metal bench that lined the back of the bus shelter. Her feet barely touched the pavement. Our true conversation began; no more guessing games. I asked her questions and interrupted at times for clarification or to steer her down a path that led deeper into the gloomy corridors of her life. Stripped of its honeysuckle sweetness, her poor Dixie childhood sounded cruel and stifling – a southern Gothic horror story of poverty and abuse. She told me about the dark days when her husband drank, and with some remorse, she spoke of her daughters – one favored over the years and another, now dead, who was often pushed aside. Her grandchildren became more than just a sum total. She gave them each an identity, and while some were left simply at that, the troubled ones had detailed stories attached to their names. Trouble at school, trouble with the law, trouble with their marriages – always with their hands held out, they chipped away at Harriet's meager nest egg until there was nothing left but a moldering mobile home and social security checks. And the deaths...the deaths were like punctuation marks. Harriet told me of her life as if she were watching a dreary, exhausted parade slowly make its way to the end. Her dead daughter waved from a dismal float decorated like a dingy nursing home. Grandchildren and great-grandchildren who had met untimely ends courtesy of illness, accident, or overdose followed behind. Harriet's old co-workers, dressed in the heavy overalls they wore as they toiled year after crushing year in a factory that made toaster ovens, smiled sadly as they marched past. "Last week Dad couldn't remember my name—can you imagine that?" Harriet said in almost a whisper, but the twinkle returned to her eye along with her waggish smile, and she said, "But I'll make it to seventy-five...that's the diamond anniversary." She had rebuilt the facade, brought back the pretense that hides reality from the glaring light, but day was long gone, and Harriet was in the dark where truth moves freely. "I pray every day that I'll make it to that anniversary...and God listens to *my* prayers," she said with an alarming defiance, but after hearing Harriet's life story I couldn't imagine what prayers had been answered over the years. I shrugged and smiled, "I'm not sure what it means or what it's worth...it's just a number, and there's nothing special about a number." Harriet's face scrunched up into a frown. "You want to wear a big orchid corsage and renew your vows at the 11:15 mass, then have a family-style dinner at dank restaurant with dark wood paneling and relish trays because after all these years and after all this shit, you have to pretend there's some reason to be happy...that every goddamn rotten moment was worth it," I said, handing the old wedding picture back to Harriet. The bus pulled up, and Harriet wiggled off of the metal bench with a hop. She hurried up the stairs as fast as her short legs allowed and took a seat. I wondered if she would turn and look out the window to acknowledge me when the bus pulled away, but she just stared ahead as I waited patiently for the next one.

HOPE: CONNIE

I'm not certain how I ended up in a pancake house restaurant seated across the table from an old woman named Connie who was wolfing down a Reuben sandwich, a cup of New England clam chowder, and a large piece of carrot cake with a thick layer of sugary white frosting as if it were the last meal she'd eat before taking a seat in the electric chair. It all began when Gus crapped in his pants.

Accidents, crime scenes, and public misfortunes, without fail, attract curious crowds of people who rubber-neck to get a better view of the carnage, catastrophe, or humiliation that unexpectedly appear to liven up their otherwise dreary day, but there's nothing compelling about human wreckage parked in a wheelchair on the patio of a nursing home. In fact, it's a fairly common sight, but the other evening I stopped to watch a nurse attend to an old man whose life was past the point of spent. I assumed it was an old man, but he was at the advanced age where gender has lost its grip on a person, so I wasn't certain if the withered figure strapped in the wheelchair and covered up with blankets despite the warm night air was male or female until I learned his name was Gus. He was so still, so sunken that I wondered if he might be dead, but then I saw the slight movement of his yellowish blood-shot eyes darting from side to side as he suddenly gasped and struggled with a dry, clattering rattle to draw in a breath. His head swiveled in slow motion, and his toothless mouth gaped in a desperate attempt to gulp down enough air to get him through to the next struggle for survival. A nurse who weigh all of 300 pounds waddled out onto the patio, sighed, and listlessly gave the old man several half-hearted taps on his back. The only urgency to be found in the situation resided in the terrified expression on the old man's face. Panic more than fear flickered across his desiccated features as he desperately tried to cling to all that was left to him: hope– hope that he would be returned to his bed in the nursing home, hope that he would have at least one more day before the end wrapped its icy cold fingers around him. Hope...no matter how miserable his life had become, he hoped for just a moment more. "Breathe," the nurse casually suggested more than compelled, then, in a voice loud enough that it could only be considered cruel, said, "Gus, you dirtied yourself again." She released the wheelchair's break with a jolt and returned the old man to his room in the Crest Haven Estates Nursing Home.

The nursing home was lit up like a low-end department store, and I could see into the windows on each of the three floors. The dining rooms were muted shades of mauve, yellow, and teal, but the residents' rooms glowed dull gray with fluorescent lights shining forlornly through plastic-backed curtains. Shapes, indistinct and stooped but recognizably human, moved slowly past the windows like the first chill breeze announcing the end of summer. Morbid fascination, or perhaps simple nosiness, got the best of me, and I found myself walking through the front doors. The Filipino nurse behind the desk on the first floor looked up and nodded with an expressionless face, then went back to watching the small TV sitting on the front counter. She saw me as just another family member, just another guest there for a dreaded visit shrouded in gloom. The common areas were styled in a way to suggest hominess, but everything looked like it had been decorated by a space alien with only a cold, confused, superficial notion of what people on Earth might consider "homey." The smell, a mixture of antiseptic cleaning agents and helplessness, was strong enough to taste, and the residents drifted aimlessly through the stink and "hominess" like sluggish tropical fish in a dangerously cold aquarium. People in wheelchairs dotted the hallways, and they slowly rocked back and forth as if they had retreated back to some long-gone time when they were far different men and women who still looked to the next day, the next five years – the future – with passion. The sound of an entertainment news show cheerfully spilled from the dining room where residents sat staring blankly at some point in the air that fell far short of the smiling effusive hostess on the TV's screen.

A strange quacking noise diverted my attention, and I turned to find an old woman dressed in a baggy pink sweat suit standing next to me. She was small and slender with very short silvery-white hair and large ill-fitting false teeth. I couldn't understand anything she said as sounds more than syllables escaped her. She gestured and pointed and shook her head in frustration until finally a few words began to form. Her name was Connie, and she became my guide through the nursing home. Connie pointed out certain residents and, with great effort, told me their names and explained each one through the people who would come to visit. Semi-comatose Helen – whose room was crowded with stuffed animals, greeting cards, and a rainbow of ruffled throw pillows – received dimly unnoticed visits from her daughter three times a week. The weary-eyed woman would sit beside her mother's bed for an hour, forty-five minutes, or sometimes less, then leave the room without looking back to return to her job, her family...a life far from the lingering horror surrounded by teddy bears and Beanie Babies. Dick had five children who would take turns to see their father on Sundays. A former Marine who served in the early years of Vietnam, his wheelchair was decorated with an incongruous shiny green, purple and yellow metallic foil pinwheel. We passed a room with a skeleton of a man propped up in bed. His eyes closed and his face twisted into a rictus grin, Charlie had recently ceased to recognize his wife on her weekly visits. Marion sat on settee next to the elevator with her visiting sister beside her. Connie held up one finger, then spread her hands apart. "Marion's sister comes once a week?" I asked, but Connie frowned, shook her head, and spread her hands wider. "Once a month?" I tried again. My companion smiled and patted my arm. Marion tugged at her housecoat, shrugged, and said to no one in particular, "Brown bears, black bears, they've been in this hemisphere for two million years." Her sister swallowed hard and smiled weakly at me before I turned away. Connie pointed to a heavy old woman sagging in a wheelchair, her head resting in her right hand, her useless left hand lying like a limp, shriveled claw in her lap. "That's Irene," Connie struggled to tell me. Irene's children would come every day, and on the weekends they would wheel her out of the nursing home for dinner at a casual restaurant just around the corner, the type of place that's popular with the lunch crowd and families. "It's nice," Connie enthused, although she had never been there herself. Connie never had any visitors of her own; no one ever came to see her, though whether she had no relatives or friends or whether they simply chose to forget about her, I wasn't sure, but she seemed to take some pleasure, even pride, in the guests who dutifully came to visit the luckier residents. The stink of processed food left too long in a microwave mixed with the odors of Pine-Sol and urine wafted from the dining room. Connie once again mentioned the restaurant around the corner and suggested that maybe I should go there sometime myself. I didn't see any point in explaining why I have no interest in tuna melts or meat loaf plates, so I simply agreed. Eventually we made our way back to the nursing station and I seized the opportunity to escape, but before I could finish my "goodbye" Connie brought The Old Hampshire Buffet restaurant to my attention for a third time, assuring me, most emphatically, that it was "very nice."

I returned Connie to the nursing home with a considerable amount of her meal spilled onto the front of her pink sweatshirt. The nurse led her down a hallway back to her room, and through a series of peeps and squawks and fractured vowels accompanied by some overly excited gestures, Connie produced the words that conveyed how nice the pancake house had been. Kindness is not one of my virtues, so why I took Connie to the restaurant with its booths, plastic laminated menus, and choice of coleslaw or sweet potato fries, I can't say. Probably I was simply taken off-guard or wanted to avoid the unpleasant scene of an old woman crying and begging and pleading as I walked out, leaving her behind. Before you accuse me of compassion, keep in mind that I did no small favor for Connie; in fact, I did her a great disservice. I gave her hope. I gave her the cruel hope that someday I would come back to visit her again, but after days pass, then weeks, her hope will become blurred and more general. She'll hope that someone, anyone will come to see her, and she'll cling to the belief that someday someone will. People spend their lives hoping for good fortune, love, or anything that's forever just out of reach – they hope for the elusive day that will never come. The absence of hope is truth. When you "face the facts" there is no room for hope. It's a lousy world, it always has been. People hope for the best when there is only worst to be had. The dread of what's next is enough to spoil even the simplest of pleasures. In the midst of a postcard-perfect summer day people hope the next day won't bring rain. Before I arrived unexpected and unannounced, Connie had long lost the hope that anyone from her happier past would come to visit in her ghastly present. No longer did she wander the halls of the nursing home expecting that someone would come to see her; she haunted the fluorescent-lit corridors with the cold understanding that she would face the wretched final act of her life alone, but she had begun to feel joy in the tiny pleasures of others. The daughters and sons and grandkids who made the unhappy trip to see Helen and Dave and Irene gave comfort to Connie – gave her troubled mind just a bit of peace. I took that from her. I burned away the comfort and carved away the peace and left her with hope.

PLAYING MUSICAL CHAIRS IN SODOM AND GOMORRAH: DALE

The beloved children's game Musical Chairs is believed to date from some time around 1875, but while the name may have been coined in the late nineteenth century, the concept is much older. I can assure you that the origin of the game is quite ancient and was first conceived during the age when philosophers from Greece and Babylon to Persia and the Far East began to spring up like introspective mushrooms spreading their spores of wisdom. Looking back upon my formidable deeds, I doubt that I would ever consider musical chairs to be my masterpiece – my *Mona Lisa*, my *Citizen Kane*, my *Revolver* – but the simple little game is nonetheless a continuing source of pride for me. One long, long ago night in the now-dead city of Miletus, I eavesdropped silently on a tedious discussion among a small group of Bronze Age know-it-alls who had come to believe that they possessed the answers to the world's most beguiling questions in their murky conjectures. The conversation took a sudden turn towards the more commonplace when my brainy companions, weary from their deep contemplations, began to complain about the generally uncivilized behavior of the city's unruly children. "All of the pointless games they play should be learning experiences," one of the philosophers said, completely unaware that his child-rearing theory was far ahead of its time. "Why is play so idle and useless? The little ones should become well-versed in the ways of the world through their games," he continued bombastically. Then he pointed across the fire to me and said, "Stranger, you sit there so quietly, brooding and listening. Do you agree? Am I correct?" "Oh yes," I answered. "Yes, children should be taught how the world works, and the sooner the better." I pondered the possibilities for a moment, collected my thoughts, and quickly pieced together the idea for a rudimentary but enriching amusement. The small group of wise men shrank back when they saw my sharp, pale white features as I leaned in from the shadows and described a game that would live through the ages and eventually become known as musical chairs. Following a short spell of silence, one of the men cleared his throat and said, "but—but in that game someone will always be subjected to rejection," and another quickly added, "I see no point other than deliberate cruelty in your—" I rose and snapped back at the prosaic Greeks, "Life is cruel! No matter how desperately you fight and shove and claw, the day will come when you're pushed aside, shut out, and tossed away like yesterday's trash. Your every waking moment, every breath you draw, is spent trying to escape the mortification, failure, and disappointment that will eventually chase you down and crush you…and that is the only philosophy you'll ever need – the most important lesson you can ever learn." Their features were frozen in stony consternation as the terrible truth settled around them. I stood in the flickering light of the small fire and briefly considered explaining my concept for dodgeball to the speechless men, but instead I melted away into the dark. Musical chairs was born in the late hours of that night now lost in antiquity, yet still to this very day children at birthday parties, in kindergarten classrooms, and at summer camps race around, cheeks flushed with despair and eyes wild with anxiety, as they battle to save themselves from being the one…rejected, shut out, and humiliated.

Musical chairs wasn't a minor stroke of my genius; it was an observation, plain and simple. The nasty little game is played out every day in office buildings and schools, amongst friends and family, in politics at both the highest and lowest levels…even at the International Mr. Leather convention. Memorial Day weekend is the official start of the summer season, and most people spend their time away from work and the daily grind by enjoying garden-variety activities such as backyard barbecues, baseball games, and fireworks displays, but Memorial Day in the city of Chicago is a far more exotic holiday thanks to the annual arrival of the International Mr. Leather circus. IML began decades ago as a gathering of like-minded fellows dressed up in motorcycle gear and various uniforms, but each edition of the social event has grown bigger and wilder, and it has now achieved major convention status in the City of Broad Shoulders. Chicago enjoys the flood of cash that sweeps in with IML, but religious and conservative groups fret and wring their hands every year over what they consider to be nothing but a sordid three-day orgy. The devout often attend religious retreats where they spend days in prayer, and I have a sneaking suspicion that more than a few conservative folks have bellied up to the buffet at an all-you-can-eat restaurant, filled their plates, and then gone back for more. Is binging on sex any different than over-indulging in God or crab cakes?

Surprisingly, debauchery on an epic scale like IML had heretofore eluded my interest, but last year I decided the annual event merited my personal attention, so I slipped into a pair of skinny black jeans and a black t-shirt and headed to the Hyatt Regency

Chicago on the Saturday night before Memorial Day. The Hyatt Regency is a huge complex that's like a small city unto itself, and upon my arrival I immediately understood why it was referred to as the IML "host hotel." I felt as if I had stepped into a teeming nest or hive of densely packed men; men in leather pants and chaps, men in harnesses, men dressed like cops and even as S.S. officers. I saw a man in full biker regalia standing beside his partner who, except for his head, was completely concealed in a large black box. How a person could travel through an airport with such a cumbersome wardrobe item seemed a mystery, but I was certain of the fact that to experience IML at its fullest I had to find my way into the middle of the crowd. Without resorting to rudeness, I pushed and wiggled through groups of guys in fireman outfits and chain link harnesses and into a horde of muscle men who chose a simple jeans-and-no-shirt look for the evening. Further and further into the thick of the mob I maneuvered myself, heading straight for the heart of darkness... or paradise, depending entirely on your point-of-view. Like a tropical reef fish that had strayed too close to an anemone, I felt grasping, groping hands reaching out all around me, but once I passed by, the arms would retreat. There was no real conviction in the clutching. Having become acclimated to the breach of my personal space and the closeness of so many people, I began to hear the bits and pieces of conversation that managed to break free from the din of overlapping voices and pounding dance music: "I dropped the price three times already. I can't afford to give the place away, so I'm staying put for a while," and, "Yeah, in my last semester. Hopefully, I can work for a year so I can afford grad school," and then, "Not so good. He didn't even recognize me last time I was there. We're trying to convince my mother that he needs to be..." No Roman orgy was unfolding around me; I observed no unchecked hedonism. What happens in Vegas stays in Vegas simply because you can't take it with you. It's only a diversion, a momentary reprieve from all the shit that is yours to keep. A Disney cruise, a weekend at Camp David, IML—there's no difference.

You're not hoping to find some time away from your job or your kids or Congress...you're trying to escape from your own life. A vacation is just a countdown to back to work; a truce is just a temporary halt to the bloodshed that will resume. Even sleep is only a fitful fleeting respite from the troubles that sit and wait patiently for you to wake. A lousy boss, a crumbling relationship, money problems...no amount of leather and attitude can keep real life from crashing the party.

I broke free of the throng and headed to a small cocktail table near one of the service bars and was surprised to find a shirtless man leaning on the table when I approached. I hadn't noticed him. "Excuse me," I said, taking a step back. "No problem," he answered amicably, "there's plenty of room." Dale from Cincinnati had reached his mid-forties – he was nice-looking, which is better than pleasant but less than good-looking and somewhat below handsome. He reminded me of one of those actors who is normally cast as an office worker in television commercials for investment products or allergy medication. From the neck down he was more impressive, and while not big, he was well-built, and he obviously put considerable effort into maintaining his fit condition, yet he seemed slightly ill-at-ease with himself. "My first time at one of these things," Dale told me, and I nodded my head. "Same here. I wanted to see what all the fuss was about." I began to explain when two twenty-something guys with the jittery, twitchy energy that never lingers past thirty walked up and set their drinks down on the table. They were same size, the same build, and, for all practical purposes, mirror images except that one had dark curly hair and the other's head was shaved. The dark haired one looked directly at Dale, appraised him without subtlety, and asked his buddy, "What do you think?" "Okay, I guess," his friend shrugged, "but he looks kind of like my dad… if my dad worked out." They both winced slightly, and the curly headed guy said, "He's probably better, you know, when it gets later." They pushed themselves away from the table and were gone, leaving me alone with Dale to deal with the uncomfortable aftermath of the encounter. He smiled a wounded smile and struggled and stammered to find words that might erase what had just happened, so I quickly pointed out a heavy-set man in leather chaps with his ample bare ass exposed. "His friends should have politely suggested pants," I observed in an attempt to cheer Dale up, but a small assemblage suddenly clustered around the fat man, and hands began to grab his sagging behind like bakers kneading dough. Singly, in twosomes and threesomes and groups of various sizes, men paraded past our table. I received a few "Hey"s and handful of "What's up?"s and even a "Nice" from the procession of strangers, but Dale remained unnoticed by one and all, and I realized that something more interesting than a festival of fucking and sucking was unfolding before me. No committee had met in secret to decide his fate for the night, no fliers had been posted with his picture and instructions to ignore him, but some intangible collective consciousness had chosen Dale, for no particular reason, to be pushed aside.

We abandoned the table, and I faded away, became like a shadow sifting unseen through the crowd as I led Dale on a terrible journey. The throng moved and surged, constantly circling through the spacious lobbies and lounge areas of the hotel, and we followed the movement and floated with the tide. The gathering guys would stop, reset, and reform with introductions exchanged, connections made, and new friendships forged. Many of the men were spectacular specimens with sculpted physiques and stunning looks, while others were unappealing and some even grotesque, although most of the attendees were no better or worse than Dale, but even among the average he found no welcome. Lurking inside everyone is the dreadful awareness that at any moment life can turn and point its cruel finger…at you. Call it fate, call it bad luck—call it whatever you wish, but no one is safe. Perplexity turned to panic, then panic became a resignation as thudding as the ceaseless disco music vibrating the floors when Dale realized that no matter how straight he stood, no matter how sincerely he smiled or intensely he glowered, on this night, through no fault of his own, when the music stopped and the seats were taken, he was the odd man out.

Dale looked relieved when I told him that I was heading out. "I bought a museum pass for tomorrow," he said as we left the Hyatt Regency. "It's gonna be a busy day, so I didn't want to stay out all night anyway." He flagged down a cab, but two guys in army fatigues rushed past as if he wasn't there and climbed into the taxi. "Are you coming back here tomorrow night?" Dale asked while he waited for the next cab. "No," I said, "I've seen enough." He looked back at the hotel, nodded, and said, "Me too. I think I'll try some of the bars up north. I checked my visitor's guide, and a few of them look kind of fun…I mean, not as intense as all this." I don't know what brought Dale from Cincinnati to the Hyatt Regency Chicago for IML – maybe boredom, too many long hours at work, or just the need to escape the numbing reality of one day after another. I'm not even sure what he expected to find, but I know he left more alone than when he arrived.

I walked down the street and tried to shake the feeling of disappointment that followed me like a mangy stray dog. The night had begun with great expectations, but I witnessed no shockingly excessive behavior, no outrageous debauchery, no extravagant sexual hijinks performed shamelessly for all to see. Flashes of nudity and eccentric costuming weren't enough to insulate IML from the intrusion of mundane and dull everyday concerns, and despite the camaraderie and sweaty bonding among the participants, life's nasty little game of musical chairs would not be denied its sacrifice – its humiliated victim. What's the point of having fun if someone isn't left out? I can only imagine what took place on floor after floor behind the rows of numbered doors lining the Hyatt Regency's hallways, but private matters are no substitute for public spectacles, and I had resigned myself to a night in which I would witness no splashy, ostentatiously unrestrained mischief when I spied a small but boisterous crowd gathered in front of an elegant, older hotel a short distance away. The group was composed of typical late-night denizens, the drunken remnants of a wedding party and a few stragglers from IML who had joined together not as individuals but as one singular entity that formed a circle around two bridesmaids locked in mortal combat. The girls held fast to each other with fistfuls of hair, and their plum-colored empire-waisted gowns blew gently in the breeze as they slowly twisted and turned, each patiently waiting to seize a moment of weakness in her foe. "Come on! Whooo!" a voice in the crowd shouted in encouragement, and one of the IML guys took a picture with his cell phone and casually showed it to a woman standing next to him. She pointed to the tiny screen and laughed. Suddenly, one of the battling bridesmaids untangled her hand from a hank of hair and slapped her enemy across the face. A cheer rose up accompanied by hoots and whistles, and a groomsman standing next to me with a rumpled shirt hanging untucked from his tuxedo pants turned and gave me a boozy two thumbs up. The desk manager, followed by a bellhop, rushed out of the hotel and waved her arms over her head at a squad car approaching the fracas on the street in a grand show of flashing lights. The crowd began to clap in unison as the cops climbed out of their car and headed towards the two young ladies who were now rolling around on the sidewalk. The groomsman held my shoulder to steady himself and said, "Outstanding!"

It was a pretty good night after all.

ANYWHERE BUT HERE: RAYMOND

I followed the crowd. More correctly, I was swept up in the surge of people heading towards a destination that held some great importance to the collective consciousness. It was late in the evening on the final Saturday night of the Auto Show, and although the annual exhibit had already been running for two full weeks, the convention center was swarmed with excited spectators. The cars looked less excited to be there. Even with the constant buffing and vacuuming, the Mercedes and BMWs and Cadillacs were beginning to show the wear and tear of a constant stream of visitors climbing in and out, slamming doors, pulling gearshifts, and turning knobs. The bread-and-butter-mobiles that carry people to and from their jobs, that run from one daily errand to another – the Hondas, Toyotas, and Fords – received far less attention than the sports cars and luxury models priced beyond the reach of most everyone who waited in line for a few minutes' time behind the wheel.

"Der it is…der it is!" an older man in a denim jacket with his gray hair slicked back like James Dean and his wallet attached to his belt with a chain shouted and pointed at a screaming yellow

Dodge Challenger with black rally stripes. "Dat's what I want, dat's da one I want!" he said as he climbed into the retro-designed model that's a near-replica of its legendary 1970 muscle car forerunner. The old man gripped the Challenger's steering wheel tightly with both hands, and for just a moment he was transported back to a time when he was young and lived in world that seemed to offer so much and asked for so little in return. I sat in as many cars as possible with my interest directed more towards the strangers who would accompany me for a few seconds than to the polished wood and appointments that all began to look pretty much the same. I was joined in a BMW by a group of young siblings who had matching straw blond hair and identical features even though they ranged in age from around five years old to eleven. They looked more like a creepy genetic experiment than a normal collection of offspring. "You have funny eyes," one of the hyperactive kids said as he pushed his way between the front seats and stared directly into my face. Often times, I would slip quietly into the back seat so I could observe the strangely mismatched parings that shared an uneasy several moments of time side-by-side in the front of the cars' cabins. A skinny woman with long, dry, bleached out hair that still clung to a bad frizzy perm around the bottom two or three inches opened the door to a $90,000 Mercedes. She wore skin-tight jeans with rhinestone designs on the back pockets and a Pabst Blue Ribbon Beer sweatshirt. Once comfortably seated in the passenger seat, she began nodding her head in a circular motion. Next to her, behind the steering wheel, was a woman who I guessed to be around 50. Dressed in crisp khaki pants with the collar of her button-down shirt poking from the top of her dove gray sweater, she was the classic vision of "old money." "Now were talkin," the skinny blonde said as she tapped her bony hand on the dashboard. The well-dressed woman shook her head, sighed, then climbed out of the car and said to her husband, "Let's go look at Acura." I stepped out of the back and took my place in the driver's seat. "I could get used to this," the skinny woman in the rhinestone jeans said, giving no indication that she was, in fact, keenly aware of the wealthy woman's rudeness. "Oh, just when you get used to it, the transmission goes," I said. The woman paused, then laughed a gritty smoker's laugh. "Ain't that the truth!" She ran her hand along the polished wood embellishment on the door and said, "It all ends up a pile of junk in the end...everything...doesn't it?" She opened the door and pulled herself out of the car.

Dream cars – waxed and polished chariots to carry you away on 18-inch chrome wheels to a time and place that's anywhere but here. I miss the old glory days of the Auto Show and the GM Motorama exhibits when the fantasy was sold with conviction. Models in ball gowns and bouffant hairdos posed on platforms with flamboyant show cars that pointed to a future no one ever believed would come true but seemed so tantalizingly idyllic. Now it's all the bottom line. Concept cars are just thinly disguised production models opening out of town before their official Broadway debut being hawked by models in business-casual attire and headsets. It's price, not works of design and technological art, that beguiles the masses now. A $60,000, $80,000, $100,000 window sticker is all that's needed to put the promise of "anywhere but here" front and center but in reach for no more than fleeting few seconds.

Three guys older than teenagers but not quite yet adults asked me to take their picture standing in front of a sparkling black metallic Camaro SS. I expected them to mug for the camera, to battle for position, strike annoying muscle poses, and otherwise cause me to harbor a quickly established dislike for them, but instead, they stood shoulder to shoulder and smiled with a sadness that made me guess they realized just how quickly the few years of youth pass by. I handed back the camera phone and said, "There you go." They stared at the tiny screen, silently regarding their moment frozen in time. A crowd was gathered around the Corvette, and I had to wait more than a few minutes before I could drop down into the passenger seat. Raymond climbed into the driver's seat next to me and closed the door. He ran his hand along the window ledge, lightly gripped the gearshift, then held onto the steering wheel with a noticeable sense of reverence...not for the car, but for the dreams that had helped him through the years, one bad day after another.

We both stepped out of the Corvette at the same time to allow others their turn in the low-slung leather seats, and Raymond took the opportunity to strike up a conversation. He knew all sorts of facts about the legendary sports car from its more humble beginnings to its fire-breathing present, but when he began to insert bits and pieces of personal story into his historical dissertation of the 'Vette, I saw that Raymond felt alone and isolated even in the Auto Show's teaming crowd. He needed someone to listen to him even if he couldn't believe they cared. Raymond followed me from one car to another; from one carpeted, video monitor-bespangled display to another. "450 horsepower," he said, pointing to a family sedan outfitted with huge wheels and an incongruously bright paint job. "It's basically a cop car package with some ground effects added on," he shrugged. Several times I spied an opportunity to disappear into the crowd, but Raymond would alert me to a poorly executed design or a headlight treatment he called "revolutionary," and I found myself patiently enduring his presence.

"It was nice meeting you," I said once we had made our way out of the hall, but before I could hail one of the waiting cabs, Raymond insisted on driving me home. "I'm heading north, too," he assured me. Raymond's gunmetal gray Toyota Corolla, bought used at CarMax, was neat but boring. It wasn't the sort of thing that inspired dreams, and at best, it only served its purpose. Once inside the car, Raymond began to give me the grinding details of his life: the divorce he still didn't understand, the foreclosure that ruined his finances, the bout of unemployment that left him doubtful of himself and suspicious of what each new day might bring…and the depression that had plagued him constantly from a young age. Beyond disappointment, beyond worry, Raymond was tired. He was exhausted; he was worn out from battling life. I stopped listening to him as the car headed north on Lake Shore Drive, and I began to slip away, to dissolve, to leave Raymond alone in his car. There were no answers I could give him, no advice or council I could offer. I could still hear him, but he no longer spoke to me, I was gone. He talked to himself, tried one more time to sort through the failures and disasters, tried to make sense of a life that never found its footing. His words filled the dark empty space that surrounded him and echoed and bounced back at him with no comfort, no gentle kindness. Even his dreams had lost their hope. I'm not certain what happened next; maybe the car skidded on a patch of ice lurking unseen on the pavement, or maybe Raymond pressed the accelerator and turned his wheel too sharply, but whatever the event, for whatever reason, the gunmetal gray Corolla took Raymond down the road that leads to anywhere but here.

I didn't feel the impact; not the first one when the car hit the guardrail, not the second one when the car crashed into the light post. All I felt was one fluid motion of the car spinning, then breaking apart around me, releasing me from the sad story of Raymond's life. Drivers screeched to a halt; some pulled over and rushed to the broken Toyota wrapped around the pole. Inside the wreck, Raymond's body looked surprisingly peaceful nestled in the deflated airbags. Traffic backed up all the way down the drive, and a crowd that looked eerily similar to the excited throng surrounding the gleaming cars at the Auto Show began to gather around the smashed Corolla. I hovered unseen like a shadow, then stepped forward and asked a young man calling 9-1-1 on his cell phone if he had seen what happened. "We were right behind him!" he said in a trembling, halting voice. His two friends stood motionless with their hands shoved into their pockets, and one turned to me and whispered in disbelief, "I saw it…he turned and drove right into the streetlight…like on purpose." The friends looked vaguely familiar– they were the three guys who had asked me to take their picture with the Camaro. They stood huddled together as if their simple physical closeness could protect them from a terrible truth. "Why would he do that?" one of the young men asked me. "Anywhere but here," I said as I noticed the hint of a smile on Raymond's still face.

THE COSTUMES WE CHOOSE: NATE

Walking past a vacant storefront that had been the longtime home to a popular movie rental chain, I noticed big purple, orange, and black signs in the windows announcing the arrival of a Halloween superstore. "Seeking energetic, dependable sales associates for temporary work, experienced or will train," the signs read, and being in the mood to engage myself in an experiment of social observation, I stopped in to inquire about a position. A heavy man in ill-fitting tight black jeans and an oversized black t-shirt with a huge image of Boris Karloff as Frankenstein's monster silk-screened on the front was busy taking plastic swords, battle axes, and cowboy hats out of cardboard boxes piled up around the store. With his grizzled long hair pulled back in a ponytail, unhealthy gray complexion, and bad teeth, it was impossible for me to guess his age. He could have been 27 or just as easily 56, and when he looked up from a box of glittery magic wands to ask if I was interested in a job, even his smoker's voice kept the mystery intact. His name was Nate, and he began to tell me a bit about the store, although beyond selling cheap costumes, make-up kits, decorations, and fake blood, I didn't really think there was that much for him to explain, but he talked at length as he continued to unpack his merchandise. Eventually he stood up – or straightened up – and in an odd way didn't look any taller than when he was bending over. I was struck by his complete lack of appealing characteristics or attractive features; however, he seemed pleasant enough. "We're already just about full as far as help goes, but I can always use some backup," he said, pushing an empty box away with his foot. I told him that I could only work evenings, but he quickly asked, "Weekends?" "Evenings," I repeated, "during the week or weekends, either way, evenings only." He frowned slightly and took a moment to regard my appearance more carefully, then smiled and said, "Oh, okay, I get it…evenings only, that's cool." He shook his head and opened a box filled with Pocahontas wigs.

Nate's black clothes formed a dark canvas for a variety of colorful touches from the florescent green of Boris' scowling face that filled the front of his shirt to his Converse All Stars splattered with pink and yellow paint and the bright purple tie holding back his ponytail. He moved around the store sliding costumes onto racks and arranging decorations with determination but no joy. "One of our biggest sellers every year," he said, holding up a scanty costume on a plastic hanger with a woman dressed as a black cat on the tag. "They all want to look like sluts, the women do," Nate said almost wearily. "We have slutty cats, slutty witches and nurses, slutty cave girls, and even our angel costumes are slutty." "I wonder why that is?" I asked, but Nate just opened another box and said, "The hell if I know, as long as they buy the shit, that's all I care about. Look at this," he said, handing me a costume that was wrapped in a sealed plastic bag. "Does that look like a fucking fairy princess to you? Who would let their kid walk around dressed like a hooker?" I glanced at the rather disturbing photograph on the package and agreed that the costume was inappropriately form-fitting for a child. "Form-fitting? Fuck!" He laughed sharply, then sighed, "We'll be sold out of them a week before Halloween gets here." Nate began to clip white lab coats made from a cheap, stiff, fire-retardant material onto hangers. "The men are different, most of them anyway," he said. "Usually they come in and buy a hat, you know, a top hat or something…and that's their costume. I don't know whether they're lazy or uptight." "Probably both," I offered. "A group of these young guys will come in acting all butch, and they'll pick up one of the zombie make-up kits…it's easy, they wear old t-shirts and jeans and the zombie shit on their faces…but sometimes one of them will sneak off, drift away from the others," Nate said, hanging the last of the mad doctor lab coats on the rack. "I'll look around the store and see him over by the *300* costumes, you know, the movie, the red cape and helmet. He'll come back later or the next day alone and buy it…that *300* shit is really popular with the closet cases." "All they need is a Speedo," I added, but Nate cut me off. "Oh, no…it comes with that, too." Nate stood back and scanned the progress he had made in the store. "Finally coming together," he said, then he turned to me. "You don't look like the type of person who needs to work in a place like this."

When does a person realize that life has dealt them a short hand, that life has cheated them? I'm not talking about bad luck or random tragedy, but rather the very nuts and bolts of a person—their basic construction. Cleaned up, groomed, and dressed to perfection, Nate would still be Quasimodo and not George Clooney, and like a chimp in a tuxedo or a bear in a tutu, Nate would look incongruous if dapperly appointed. To my eyes he may have appeared sloppy, disheveled, and haphazardly clothed, but Nate had carefully constructed a personal environment to surround himself with. Everything was chosen not to mask how life had so cruelly sculpted him, but rather to make everything seem correct, intentional. His trappings insulated him from the disappointment of trying to compete or otherwise fit in with life's more pleasing work. Nate had chosen his costume carefully; most people do. Our decisions aren't based solely on physical dimensions and contours, though. Rival politicians scrounging for votes on the campaign trail make personal appearances dressed in identical "casual Friday" attire. Ambition is the only attribute they share, but that's enough for them to costume themselves in the same singular manner so as to appear "regular" to the everyday people they are in fact so remote from. Not everyone makes the wise choice; some lack the self-awareness to view themselves in the proper context, and the results are not pretty. Several decades ago, a never very funny dumb blond comedienne was considered a sex symbol, but now with her affected baby voice, jowly face, and Clarabelle couture, she just looks old, fat, and stupid as she wanders through the badlands of cable news and the Internet babbling about Jesus and complaining about gays. Young pop stars wrap themselves in "gangsta" attire and mark themselves up with a plethora of bad tattoos in a creepy attempt to gain some street-cred maturity in the absence of real talent after they emerge from the career killing days of puberty. Does anyone think your father with his sleeveless Lynyrd Skynyrd t-shirt and biker boots is cool? Misshapen Nate is a bit grotesque and somewhat unappetizing in appearance, but he transformed himself into the type of scroungy work of art that never goes out of style. He understood that in this cruel world, he'd better turn himself into the carefully crafted joke before someone else took the pleasure.

I never returned to the Halloween emporium. I didn't need to sell make-up kits and felt hats for a week or two to see that, like the song says, every day is Halloween – a constant parade of costumes meant to drape what life doled out or to create the illusion of a reality that's a necessary means to an end. "You don't look like the type of person who needs to work in a place like this," Nate had said, sizing me up. His observation was correct although he knew not a thing about me. I have always chosen my own costumes very carefully.

PARALLEL LINES: ALEXIOS

I'm not a nostalgic creature who pines for yesteryear or a bygone day. I don't look back on any particular age with maudlin longing, but even a heartless fiend such as myself isn't completely immune to the gravitational pull of the past, and recently a nondescript little vase caused me to become consumed by vivid memories of a time that flourished thousands of years before Mark Antony met his match at Actium.

The extensive collection of ancient Assyrian artifacts were dramatically illuminated in long glass cases lining the museum's darkened exhibit hall, and a crowd of spectators snaked around a path mapped out by a black nylon version of the classic velvet rope to view the bits and pieces of antiquity unearthed, cleaned up, and put on public display. Small, simply designed cards gave historical weight to the assembled items, whether grand or modest; many of them were things of exceptional beauty while others were no more than jagged shards of broken pottery or scraps of dried, frayed textiles. People moved slowly through the exhibit in hushed reverence for relics from an age so distant it defied their reasonable comprehension – physical reminders of life's overwhelming scope and their own tiny speck of space in this endless enterprise. I viewed the show of history in a far different manner; for me it was a musty trip down Memory Lane where I paused in front of an oddly familiar-looking tiny vase set upon a simple rectangular white pedestal. My vision momentarily blurred, and the small vessel's cracks and chips healed over as its faded pigments returned to their original vibrancy. Dusk cast its burnt orange glow over Kalhu's teeming marketplace, and an anxious potter tried to make one more sale before packing up for the night. "The price is outrageous," I said flatly, turning the small vase over in my pale undead hands. "Look at it!" the artisan exclaimed with an arch sense of indignation. "The shape, the proportion – perfection! One-of-a-kind, you won't see anything like this..." "I see at least a dozen more exactly like it right there in your stall," I said as I handed the vase back to the old man and made my way into the gathering darkness. My reflection, impassive and ageless, floated on the glass that protected the vase I had held one evening countless centuries ago. An elderly woman took a pair of glasses from her purse, put a hand on her husband's shoulder, and leaned in for a closer look at the old vessel. "Remarkable," she said to him. "I wonder what people were like back then." Her husband shrugged and grunted, "Barely civilized," then pushed his way past me to the next glass case.

The exhibit's largest piece was a sizable fragment of wall with the remains of a fresco lit by a series of tiny spotlights suspended from nearly invisible thread-thin wires. "Assyrian demon, identity unknown," the woman's husband read from the card describing the evil spirit rendered on the broken section of wall. "I wouldn't want to meet him in a dark alley!" the man laughed as he captured the demon with his iPhone's camera. "Oh, Jesus, no!" his wife shuddered, then giggled. The couple turned to me, but their smiles quickly faded and were replaced with uncomfortable expressions pieced together from an intangible dread mixed with confusion. The woman lightly tugged her husband's sleeve as they moved on to another artifact, and I found myself face-to-face with my own painted image. Typically, the ancient cultures represented my likeness as flamboyantly monstrous flights of fancy with huge orb-like eyes, gnarled claws, and long, curved fangs, but preserved for all time, climate controlled behind shatter-resistant bullet-proof glass, an eerily accurate and realistic rendering of my face was painted onto the old piece of stone. I stared at the deep-set cruel, black eyes and the sharp, unfeeling features as they coldly stared back at me like a mirror image. You can't reclaim the past, nor can you escape it. Good or evil, right or wrong, "I could have…", "I should have…", or "Remember when…", the past is a shadow that will follow you to the grave.

KA-BOOM! Boston's venerable marathon will forever be remembered for an explosive few seconds, and within days of that defining mayhem, Dzhokhar Tsarnaev's curly-haired boy-band features became the face of a demon painted in pixels on computer screens and plasma TVs everywhere. He's an historical artifact now, a relic, evil preserved for posterity, a superstar of the dark side. His classmates and acquaintances were quick to paint a picture of a normal, well-adjusted teenager who wrestled, smoked weed, tweeted with earnest conviction, and listened to hip hop music, but they were puzzled and wondered why they were never able to see the real Dzhokhar lurking beneath the carefully created veneer of a normal collage kid. In fact, what they saw *was* the real deal Dzhokhar Tsarnaev. True life Jekyll and Hydes are more common that you'd think. Richard Nixon was a scoundrel as well as a devoted family man. Every Christmas, Andy Warhol spooned out slop to the homeless in a soup kitchen, but he famously treated the denizens of The Factory as human props. Genius record producer Phil Spector is currently serving a life sentence for murder, and for what it's worth, Chairman Mao was an accomplished dancer and a charming host. Parallel lines. Good and evil run through everyone like parallel lines that travel the same track but never intersect…bookends, two sides of the coin.

I'm a monster, through and through, in nature and in deed. My machinations and schemes have left a trail of wars, revolutions, shattered lives, and seething cultural divides listing bitterly in my wake, but over the course of my exceptionally long existence the rules of mathematics alone would suggest that I must have displayed a generous spirit or a good heart once or twice, although I'd need some time to recall any concrete examples of my rectitude. No one is all bad, not even me – parallel lines – but those parallel lines wind and curve side-by-side and form a question mark that lingers menacingly overhead. A question mark causes confusion and discomfort, and, more importantly, it leads to self-doubt and forces you to take a closer look at your own squirming, slimy self. Some of the most profoundly disturbing images from World War II are the strange home movies of Hitler playing fetch with his German Shepherd, Blondi. The happy despot is seen tossing a stick to the frolicking dog as the darkest hours of the war rage far below his lofty alpine getaway. Most view the weird little films as further proof of Hitler's all-consuming evil – a joyful, gloating Führer celebrating his own madness – but the reality is far more difficult to grasp, much less accept. Those flickering images depict nothing more than the flip side of the Nazi dictator: a mundane man enjoying time with his beloved pet. When the grisly handiwork of serial killer John Wayne Gacy was hauled out of the crawl space beneath his modest ranch house on live TV, a stunned nation immediately began to read evil intent in the creepy clown costume he wore to entertain children at birthday parties. His many charitable endeavors were suddenly viewed as a clever camouflage for his true unspeakable nature. Someone who could strangle nearly forty young men and leave their remains to fester just below his own living room couldn't possibly exhibit true generosity or a genuinely lighthearted fondness for captivating little ones in the guise of a clown...or could he? There's that question mark once again stirring up the mud in your mind. If a notorious psychopath can have a good side, then how dreadful is your own bad side?

"He looks like he'd be totally mean...like, you know, seriously evil mean," a high school girl said to her friends as they leaned forward to get a closer look at my portrait painted on the fragment of wall in the glass case. "He's scarier than the monster demons," another one of the girls added with a pop of her gum. Whether out of morbid curiosity or a perverted sense of vanity, I can't be certain, but for whatever personal compulsion, I lingered before the star attraction of the museum's ancient Assyrian exhibit as one after another visitor stepped up, appraised my countenance, and summed me up in a manner that could never be described as pleasant. "Soulless," "bloodless," and "hateful" were the most benign descriptors attached to my expressionless face. A man in his early forties dressed in plaid shorts from Gap, sandals, and a t-shirt imprinted with the logo of a prestigious Ivy League school studied the painted narrative on the fresco, then consulted his program with a frown. "Fascinating," he said, more to himself than to his friend. "All of the other characters are illustrated with the typical beastly attributes normally associated with the various demons of the era," he said, sweeping his hand around the general direction of the featured artifact. "But that one," he pointed an accusatory finger squarely at my image, "that one is a true portrait, almost a snapshot." "He looks like a vampire," the man's friend said with a laugh. "Absolutely vampiric," Professor Know-It-All confirmed his companion's observation. "And that legend resonates all the way back to the farthest reaches of history." The man folded his arms across his chest and shook his head. "It's completely out of place with the rest of the painting in style, composition, and symbolically as well. It's almost a warning. I wonder who he was…or is?" Both men smiled and moved on to the next preserved, perfectly presented piece of crumbling civilization.

As the museum prepared to close for the night, I was left alone with my painted self in the darkened exhibit hall. I will never claim to be handsome, but neither am I homely. I'm too exotic-looking to be ordinary, although I can easily lose myself in a crowd, yet my features rendered in pigment on a cracked facade inspired universal fear and loathing from all who viewed it. I doubt it was the angular lines of my jaw and nose that spooked the museum's guests, but rather the true character exposed in the meticulous details of my eyes and the unnerving blank expression on my face that burrowed into a troubling spot deep inside everyone who viewed the fresco. The truth be told, I painted my own self-portrait long, long before an anonymous artist touched his brush to stone. He left his painting for history's examination, conjecture, and judgment while I carry my work of art with me every day, year after year, century after century. "He looks just like you!" the museum guard said. The young guard, a college student moonlighting for a few extra bucks, smiled and continued quickly, "I meant it as a compliment. It's pretty cool, actually." "Yes," I said, turning back to the ancient chunk of wall. "It certainly is."

ABOUT THE AUTHOR

His reputation is legendary. Some of the ancient peoples tried to understand him – to explain him as best they could – and so to them he became the fearsome demons of their shared nightmares. To the Assyrians he was Rabisu, to the Persians he was Asto Vidatu, and it's been said that he inspired the Hebrew fable of the great fallen angel. Some have told fantastic stories about his mystical origin that claim he was born of the darkness itself, but his beginning was far more ordinary. He arrived into the world in the typical fashion and lived an unremarkable life until he became a young man, and then, in a single dark moment, everything changed. He came from the Peloponnese in the days long before the Greek's culture rose on elegant columns to Olympus, and to whomever has made his acquaintance, from the fog of antiquity through the rise and fall of civilizations to this time we call our own, he has always introduced himself simply as Alexios.

Alexios is currently on an extended sabbatical from meddling in history's affairs and now occupies his time observing life, composing essays, and writing his popular online advice column.

WWW.IALEXIOS.COM